CONTENTS

UNIT 1

Tools for Solving Math Problems

UNIT 2

Division

UNIT 3

Adding and Subtracting Fractions and Decimals

UNIT 4

Multiplication and Division of Fractions and Decimals

Glossary

Program Consultant
William F. Tate
Edward Mallinckrodt Distinguished University Professor
Washington University, St. Louis

Image credits can be found on page 261.

ISBN-13: 978-0-7854-6604-8
ISBN-10:   0-7854-6604-5
2 3 4 5 6 7 8 9 10 12 11 10 09

1-800-992-0244
www.pearson.com

UNIT 1
Tools for Solving Math Problems

MATH STRATEGIES

Learn **PROBLEM-SOLVING STRATEGIES** and how to apply them to solve real-world problems.

VOCABULARY

PROBLEM-SOLVING
WORDS:
Know them!
Use them!
Learn all about them!

The Four-Step
Problem-Solving Plan
1. Read   3. Solve
2. Plan   4. Check

The Four-Step Problem-Solving Plan

Step 1: Read	Step 2: Plan	Step 3: Solve	Step 4: Check
Make sure you understand what the problem is asking.	Decide how you will solve the problem.	Solve the problem using your plan.	Check to make sure your answer is correct.

When you are given a problem to solve, having a plan makes the task easier.
The Four-Step Problem-Solving Plan is a useful tool to help you solve math problems.

Step 1: Read

It is very important to read the problem carefully. Try to answer the following questions once you have read the problem.

- What do you know about the problem?
- What is the question in the problem?
- What facts are given in the problem?

If you do not understand some of the words in the problem, you can look them up in a dictionary or the glossary of your textbook.

Read the problem below. Restate the problem in your own words in the space below. Underline the question and circle any facts that could help you answer it.

1. During the summer, 1,238 children are at Camp Hideaway. There are 562 boys at the camp. Today, 339 children went swimming, and 123 of them were girls. How many girls are in camp? How many boys did not go swimming?

   _____

   _____

Step 2: Plan

Once you know what the problem is asking, you need to plan how to solve it. Ask:

- Have you solved a similar problem before?
- What problem-solving strategies can you use?

Problem-solving strategies are ways you can set up and solve a problem. In this example, you might want to look for clue words that can tell you what operation to use.

2. Write your plan for solving the problem. Make sure to explain all the steps you will take to get your answer.

   _____

   _____

   _____

   _____

Step 3: Solve

To solve the problem, follow the plan you made in Step 2. As you solve, ask:

- Are you following each step of your plan?
- Do you need to change your plan?
- Do you need to try another problem-solving strategy?

It is okay to change your plan if it does not solve the problem.

Make sure to keep a record of everything you did as you solved the problem. This is also known as showing your work. It can help you identify what you did wrong and what you did right as you move on to the next step.

3. Show your work in the space below. Circle your final answer.

_____

_____

Step 4: Check

After you have solved the problem, check your answer. Think about the following questions while you check your answer.

- Have you answered the right question?
- Did you make any mistakes as you followed the steps of your plan?
- Does your answer make sense? Is it reasonable?
- Can you solve it another way and get the same answer?

Reviewing your work once you have finished can help catch any simple mistakes you may have made.

4. As you check your answer, write your thoughts in the space below. Also write down any questions you may have about the four-step problem-solving plan. Discuss these questions with a classmate or your teacher.

_____

_____

_____

Use the Four-Step Problem-Solving Plan to solve the problem below. Follow the steps shown to you in this lesson. Write your plan on a separate sheet of paper. Write your answer below.

5. Dennis wants to buy a mountain bike for $400.00. He saved $187.00. For his birthday, his grandmother gives him $25.00. How much does Dennis still need before he can buy the bike?

_____

_____

_____

Draw a Picture or Use a Model

VOCABULARY

expression: a mathematical statement including numbers and symbols

physical model: a real-life representation of an object

strategy: a plan or way of doing something

A **strategy** is a plan or a way of doing something. Problem-solving strategies help you organize the information you need to solve a problem. A useful strategy is **Draw a Picture or Use a Model.**

Drawing a picture can help you better understand the problem. For example, drawing out the following problem can help you "see" all the bottles.

Read: Tammy and Frank are both in the Environmental Club. Today they collected five bottles. Yesterday, they collected eight bottles. How many bottles did they collect?

What do you know? They collected five bottles and eight bottles.

What do you need to find out? How many bottles did they collect?

Plan: Draw a picture to show the bottles. Count them.

Solve: There are thirteen bottles.

Check: $5 + 8 = 13$

This drawing also shows the **expression** $5 + 8$.

---

1. **Read:** The Corner Market sells fresh fruit each day. Today, there are 14 pears and 29 apples. How many pieces of fruit does the Corner Market have for sale today? Hint: Draw a picture below to help you solve.

What do you know? _____

What do you need to find out? _____

Plan: _____

Solve: _____

Check: _____

The Use a Model strategy can either refer to a **physical model** or a model on paper. One example of a physical model is base ten blocks. Base ten blocks come in single blocks, rods of 10, and flats of 100.

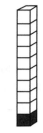

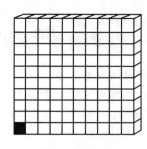

1 single block   one rod of 10 blocks   one flat of 100 blocks

2. **Read:** Andrew had a baseball card collection of 679 cards. He sold 370 cards. How many cards were left?
   Hint: Draw a model below to help you solve.

What do you know? _____

What do you need to find out? _____

Plan: _____

_____

Solve: _____

Check: _____

3. When is it useful to use the Draw a Picture or Use a Model strategy?

_____

_____

4. Is there anything you do not understand when using this strategy?

_____

_____

_____

Find a Pattern

VOCABULARY

pattern: objects, designs, or numbers that change in a specific way

rule: a description of the way a pattern works

Patterns are objects, designs, or numbers that repeat or change in a certain way. The **Find a Pattern** strategy can help you solve problems where the answer can be found by filling in the pattern.

You need to look at the pattern carefully and decide how it was created. This is the **rule** of the pattern, which describes how the pattern works. With numbers, the rule might be "subtract 3" or "divide by 2." With shapes, the rule might describe a repeating pattern of shapes, such as "triangle, square, then circle." To understand the pattern, you must find the rule.

Read: Fill in the missing numbers in the pattern below.

8, 13, 18, _____, 28, _____, _____

What do you know? There are three numbers given in the pattern: 13, 18, and 28.

What do you need to find out? Find the three missing numbers.

Plan: Look for a pattern by seeing how the numbers change. Use this pattern to fill in the missing numbers.

Solve: 18 − 13 = 5, so the numbers increase by 5. The missing numbers are 23 (18 + 5), 33 (28 + 5), and 38 (33 + 5).

Check: 23 is 5 more than 18, so the numbers fit the pattern.

1. **Read:** Fill in the missing numbers. Explain what the pattern is.

225, 200, _____, 150, 125, _____, _____

What do you know? _____

What do you need to find out? _____

Plan: _____

_____

Solve: _____

_____

Check: _____

The pattern below is called the Fibonacci (fē´ bə na´ chē) sequence.

1, 1, 2, 3, 5, 8, 13 …

2. What is the rule for this pattern?

_____

_____

3. What is the next number in the sequence? How do you know?

_____

_____

Patterns can also be found in pictures or a series of shapes. For example, the shapes can repeat in a certain order or change the number of sides. You must look carefully to find how the shapes repeat or change.

4. Find the missing shapes. Write the rule below. Then, draw the missing shapes on the lines in the pattern.

▲ ■ ● ▲ _____ ● _____ ■ ● _____

Rule: _____

_____

_____

5. On your own paper, draw a pattern using combinations of numbers or objects. Then exchange it with a partner who will find and complete the pattern.

6. Is there something about finding patterns you do not understand?

_____

_____

_____

Make a List

VOCABULARY

combination: a group of objects in which order does not matter

tree diagram: a diagram that shows possible combinations branching off each other

When reading, lists are an excellent tool to help you understand the text. In math, the **Make a List** strategy helps you see information in an organized way. For example, lists help you keep track of the possible **combinations** of items. Lists can also help you keep track of possible outcomes. See the example below for one way to use a list.

Read: To use the juice machine, you must have quarters, dimes, or nickels. A large juice costs $2.00. Jerome has enough money, but he only has quarters and nickels. In how many ways can Jerome make up the $2.00 he will need to get a large juice?

What do you know? A large juice costs $2.00; Jerome will use only quarters ($0.25, or 25 cents) and nickels ($0.05, or 5 cents).

What do you need to find out? How many ways Jerome can make up $2.00 using only quarters and nickels.

Plan: I can make a list of all the different possible combinations of quarters and nickels that make $2.00. The list should start with the most possible quarters Jerome could use and then go down by one.

Solve: Possible combinations:

1. 8 quarters
2. 7 quarters, 5 nickels
3. 6 quarters, 10 nickels
4. 5 quarters, 15 nickels
5. 4 quarters, 20 nickels
6. 3 quarters, 25 nickels
7. 2 quarters, 30 nickels
8. 1 quarter, 35 nickels
9. 40 nickels

Jerome can make up the $2.00 in nine different ways.

Check: Use multiplication and addition to check that each set of coins equals $2.00.

1. **Read:** For her lunch, Tara has a choice of a ham, turkey or salami sandwich with either swiss or cheddar cheese. How many sandwich choices does Tara have, if she has to choose one type of meat and one cheese for her sandwich?

One way to help create a list is to make a **tree diagram.** This diagram shows possible combinations "branching off" like a tree. Here is a tree diagram for this problem.

| Ham | — Swiss |
| | — Cheddar |

| Turkey | — Swiss |
| | — Cheddar |

| Salami | — Swiss |
| | — Cheddar |

What do you know? _____

_____

What do you need to find out? _____

_____

Plan: _____

_____

_____

Solve: _____

Check: _____

_____

2. **Read:** How many different three-digit numbers can you make using the digits 6, 7, and 8?

What do you know? _____

What do you need to find out? _____

Plan: _____

Solve: _____

Check: _____

3. Joel has four letters in his name. How many combinations of two letters can he make? Show how you solved the problem.

_____

_____

_____

4. When would you use the Make a List strategy to solve a problem?

_____

5. Write a word problem that you should solve by making a list. Then let a partner solve it.

_____

_____

Graphic Organizers

Graphic organizers are used to arrange information in a way that makes it easy to understand. You can use a graphic organizer to display information from an article or a word problem.

A **Venn diagram** is used to compare and contrast items or ideas. Draw two circles that partly overlap. These circles represent what you want to compare. List the characteristics of one in the left circle. List the characteristics of the other in the right circle. List the characteristics they share in the area where the circles overlap.

Addition combining numbers to find their sum

Both mathematical operations

Subtraction finding the difference between two numbers

Use a **concept map** when recording supporting details of a main topic. The topic is written in a center box or circle. The supporting details are written in circles or boxes connected to the topic.

Addition	Subtraction
Mathematical operations	
Multiplication	Division

For sequencing, writing steps, or creating a timeline, the **flowchart** is an excellent organizer. The arrows show how the boxes "flow" from one to the next.

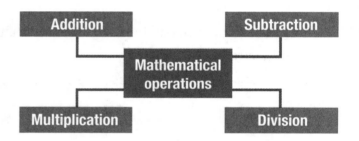

Step 1: Read	Make sure you understand what the problem is asking.
Step 2: Plan	Decide how you will solve the problem.
Step 3: Solve	Solve the problem using your plan.
Step 4: Check	Check to make sure your answer is correct.

A **three-column chart** is a good way to organize your thoughts about a new topic. In the first column, list what you know about the topic. In the second column, list the things you want to know about the topic. In the third column, list what you learned from the reading.

What I know	What I want to know	What I learned

Use graphic organizers to answer the following questions.

1. On a separate piece of paper, draw a Venn Diagram that compares numbers divisible by 2 and numbers divisible by 3. Fill in at least three numbers in each section.

2. Read a short article from a newspaper or magazine. What is the main topic of this article?

   _____

   List five supporting details. Then use these details to create a concept map on a separate sheet of paper.

   _____

   _____

   _____

   _____

   _____

3. The following steps describe the strategy for dividing $54 \div 3$. Number the steps in order from one to four. Then, on a separate sheet of paper, write the steps as a flowchart.

   _____ Write 1 above the bar and 3 underneath the 5; subtract 3 from 5 and write 2 under the next bar.

   _____ See how many times 3 goes into 5.

   _____ Write 8 above the bar.

   _____ Bring down the 4 and see how many times 3 goes into 24.

4. Create a three-column chart. Title the chart *Multiplication and Division as Inverse Operations.* Then list the things you know about the topic in the first column. In the second column, list the things you want to know and hope to learn by reading about this concept. After you read, write what you did learn in the third column.

Try a Simpler Form of the Problem

What you already know about a topic can help you understand what you read. Math is like that, too. Often in problem solving you are asked a difficult question. It becomes easier to answer when you think about what you already know about part of it. You can solve a simpler part of the problem and use that answer to solve the rest.

Read: Newville has 79,998 people. Centerville has 50,818 people. One-fifth of Newville residents have library cards, while one-third of Centerville residents have library cards. Which city has the larger number of library users?

What do you know? I know the populations of Newville (79,998) and Centerville (50,818). I know that one-fifth ($\frac{1}{5}$) of Newville residents have library cards and one-third ($\frac{1}{3}$) of Centerville residents have them.

What do you need to find out? The actual number of library card holders in each city.

Plan: I can solve a simpler form of the problem by rounding and dividing the populations by 1,000. Then I will use these simpler forms of the numbers to solve. I will multiply the answer by 1,000.

Solve: I can simplify the problem by rounding the populations to the nearest thousand and taking away the last three zeros. Then it will be easier to multiply by the fractions (or divide by their denominators).

Newville	Centerville
79,998 rounded = 80 thousand	50,818 rounded = 51 thousand
$80 \times \frac{1}{5}$ (or 80 ÷ 5) = 16	$51 \times \frac{1}{3}$ (or 51 ÷ 3) = 17
Multiply by 1,000: **16,000 library card holders**	Multiply by 1,000: **17,000 library card holders**

Therefore, Centerville has the larger number of library users.

Check: Newville: 16,000 × 5 = 80,000, which is 79,998 rounded to the nearest thousand.
Centerville: 17,000 × 3 = 51,000, which is 50,818 rounded to the nearest thousand.

---

1. **Read:** In a recent election, 1 out of 15 voters accidentally damaged their ballots. The total number of ballots cast in the election was 404,996. Did the number of damaged ballots surpass 20,000?

What do you know? _____

What do you need to find out? _____

Plan: _____

_____

Solve: _____

_____

_____

Check: _____

2. A company makes 32,000 greeting cards per month. About $\frac{1}{8}$ of the cards, or 4,000 per month, are congratulations cards for the birth of a new baby. About $\frac{1}{16}$ of the cards are sympathy cards. How many sympathy cards are made per month? Explain how you can use a simpler form of the problem to solve.

_____

_____

_____

_____

3. Factory A makes 1,250,000 hand tools in one year. Factory B makes 250,000 hand tools in the same span of time. How many times more tools does Factory A produce annually than Factory B? Explain how you can use a simpler form of the problem to solve.

_____

_____

_____

_____

_____

4. The area of a soccer field is the same as the area of 20 gymnastics mats. A gym mat has a length of 15 feet and a width of 6 feet. What is the area of the soccer field? Explain how you can use a simpler form of the problem to solve.

_____

_____

_____

_____

_____

5. Describe how you created a simpler form of the problem in problem 3.

_____

_____

6. In problem 4, what was your first step, and how did you know you needed to find it first?

_____

_____

 Make a Table or a Chart

A chart is a way of organizing and displaying information. Different types of charts include flowcharts, graphs, and tables.

A table is made up of information such as words and numbers organized into rows and columns. Rows run across a table and columns run up and down. The heading or label of each column helps explain how the information is organized. The title explains what information is in the table.

Title Students in Three Different Classes

Columns

Boys	Girls	Total
15	18	33
8	12	20
17	5	22

Rows

Tables can be used to find patterns. If you can find a pattern, you can make the table larger to continue the pattern. You can list the information you know, and fill in the information you don't know.

Read: An oriental rug pattern has twice as many red threads as purple threads. One rug has 80 red threads, one has 40, and another has 30 red threads. What is the total number of threads in each rug?

What do you know? There are 80 red threads in one rug, 40 in another rug, and 30 in another. There are twice as many red threads as purple in every rug.

What do you need to find out? The total number of threads in each rug.

Plan: Make a table or chart to display the number of threads for each color. Read the chart and find the number of each color thread. Then add to find the total number of threads.

Solve:

Rug	Number of Red Threads	Number of Purple Threads	Total Number of Threads
A	80	40	120
B	40	20	60
C	30	15	45

80 red ÷ 2 = 40 purple threads
40 red ÷ 2 = 20 purple threads
30 red ÷ 2 = 15 purple threads

Add to find the total number of threads in each rug.

Check: For each rug, multiply the number of purple threads by 2. In each instance, the product should be the number of red threads.

1. A survey shows the number of pets that students have: 10 students have cats, 6 have dogs, 2 have birds, and 4 do not have any pets. Make a table that displays the results of the survey. Find the total number of students in the class.

   _____

2. In Rockwell Apartments, there are 12 apartment units on the first floor, 14 on the second floor, and 8 on the third floor. At Meldon Hill, there are 30 apartments on both the first and second floors, and 40 on the third floor. Make a table and find the total number of apartments in each building.

   _____

Tables can also be used to display the information you collect in a survey. Use what you have learned about tables to solve the problem below.

3. Two art classes are making sculptures. Each student has a choice of paper, wood, or clay. In Mrs. Lopez's class, 10 students chose paper, 8 chose wood, and 3 chose clay. In Mr. Gallagher's class, 4 chose paper, 12 chose wood, and 6 chose clay. Make a table to show the choices. What is the total number of sculptures in each class?

   _____

4. When is the strategy of making a table or a chart useful?

   _____
   _____
   _____
   _____
   _____

 Guess, Check, and Revise

VOCABULARY

perimeter: the distance around the outside of a shape

When you guess what might happen next in a story, you are predicting. If your prediction is incorrect, you can change it and try a new one until you find one that works. The **Guess, Check, and Revise** problem-solving strategy works the same way. You guess a possible answer. Then you try it to see if it is the correct choice. If it is not the correct choice, you can change it and try again.

Read: Jordan wants to put tile on the floor of his bedroom, which measures 8 feet by 12 feet. Boxes of tiles come with 20 tiles in each box. Each tile is 1 square foot. How many boxes of tiles should he buy?

What do you know? The dimensions of Jordan's room are 8 ft × 12 ft. There are 20 tiles in a box. Each tile has an area of 1 square foot.

What do you need to find out? What is the area of Jordan's room? How many boxes of tiles does he need to cover this area?

Plan: I can guess and check. If my guess is incorrect, I can guess again.

Solve: The area of the room is 8 feet × 12 feet = 96 ft². I guess that Jordan can buy 4 boxes of tiles.

Check: I will divide 96 by 20 to see if 4 boxes of tiles will be enough.

Revise: $96 \div 20 = 4.8$. Since $4.8 > 4$, Jordan will need to buy 5 boxes of tiles.

---

1. **Read:** The product of two numbers is 126. The numbers are 39 digits apart. What are the two numbers?

What do you know? _____

What do you need to find out? _____

Plan: _____

_____

Solve: _____

Check: _____

Revise: _____

_____

---

2. The sum of two numbers is 70. The difference of these numbers is 14. What are the two numbers?

_____

One type of problem that often uses the Guess, Check, and Revise strategy is a **perimeter** problem. Perimeter is the distance around the outside of a shape. The perimeter of a rectangle is the sum of its sides. A rectangle has two sides that are one length and two sides that are another length. A square has four sides that are all the same length.

3. **Read:** The area of Louisa's rectangular garden is 42 square feet. What is the length and what is the width of her garden?

What do you know? _____

What do you need to find out? _____

Plan: _____

Solve: _____

Check: _____

Revise: _____

_____

Are there other possibilities? _____

_____

4. A square has an area of 121 feet. What is the length and width of the square?

_____

Are there other possibilities? Why or why not?

_____

5. What other strategy could you use to help you answer questions 3 and 4?

_____

_____

_____

6. What is one disadvantage of the Guess, Check, and Revise strategy?

_____

_____

_____

Graphic Organizers

Math graphic organizers can help you compare information.

A **bar graph** uses rectangular bars to compare information. The length or height of each bar represents an amount. The **scale** on the side of the graph gives an amount for each height or length.

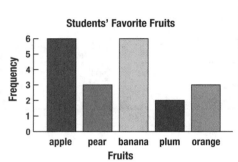

Students' Favorite Fruits

Circle graphs are used to show parts of a whole. Each piece in a circle graph is a different part of the whole. Think of a pizza that is cut into eight slices. Each piece is one-eighth of the whole pizza. When pieces of a circle graph are different sizes, they show different amounts.

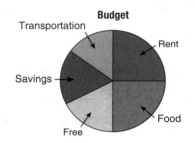

Budget

Coordinate grids are used to display pairs of numbers called **ordered pairs.** Each ordered pair names one point on the coordinate grid. Marking a point on a coordinate grid is also known as **plotting** the point. The points you plot can represent lines, shapes, or general information.

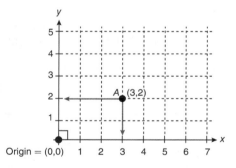

Use graphic organizers to organize information and solve the following problems.

1. Miriam made a bar graph of the change she found in her bag. How many times more nickels did she have than quarters?

_____

_____

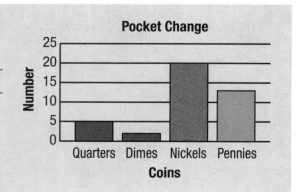

Pocket Change

2. Javier surveyed his classmates to find out their favorite types of fruit. They could choose only one from apples, oranges, pears, peaches, and grapes. He displayed the information in a circle graph.

If Javier surveyed 100 students, how many said they liked peaches best?

_____

_____

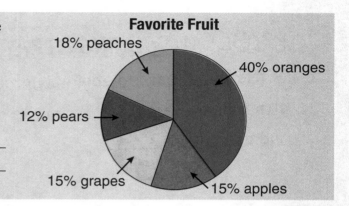

Favorite Fruit

18% peaches

40% oranges

12% pears

15% grapes

15% apples

3. Plot these points on a coordinate grid. Do they all fall on the same straight line?

(0, 0), (5, 6), (4, 4)

_____

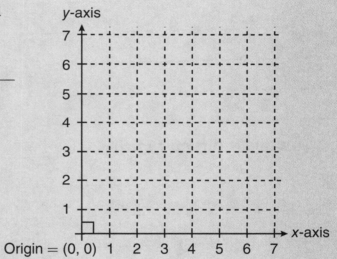

4. When you want to display the temperature on various days of the week in a graph, which graph is best to use, a bar graph or a circle graph? Why?

_____

_____

5. When you want to graph how much time you spent on different activities during the 24 hours that make up a whole day, which graph would you use, a bar graph or a circle graph? Why?

_____

_____

6. Other than a map, what is another example of a coordinate grid?

_____

_____

Unit 1 Reflection

Review and Record What You Learned

PROBLEM-SOLVING STRATEGIES

In this unit, I learned about six problem-solving strategies. The easiest for me to remember and use is

$\sqrt{25}$

$$\begin{array}{r} 93 \\ +620 \\ \hline 713 \end{array}$$

π

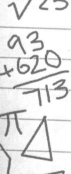

The most difficult strategy is

I do not understand

UNIT 2
Division

MATH SKILLS & STRATEGIES
After you learn the basic **SKILLS,** the real test is knowing when to use each **STRATEGY.**

READING STRATEGY
Learn the steps to good **Summarizing.**

AMP LINK MAGAZINE
You Do the Math and Math Projects: After you read each magazine article, apply what you know in real-world problems.
Fluency: Make your reading smooth and accurate, one tip at a time.

VOCABULARY
MATH WORDS:
Know them!
Use them!
Learn all about them!

CONNECTIONS
You own the math when you make your own connections.

Reading Comprehension Strategy: Summarizing

How to Summarize

Step 1:	Step 2:	Step 3:	Step 4:
Identify the **topic:** Ask, *Who or what is this about?*	Identify the **main idea:** Ask, *What is the main thing the writer is saying about the topic?*	Identify the **important details:** Ask, *What details are needed to understand the main idea?*	Use the main idea and important details to **summarize.**

Step 1: Identify the Topic

When you summarize, you identify the most important things in the section you are reading. First, look for the topic. The **topic** is a word or phrase that answers the question, *Who or what is this about?* Good summaries do not include a lot of extra facts. What is the topic of the paragraph below?

> Sing some words from your favorite song. How many notes can you sing at once? Just one—you cannot make two sounds at once. However, some people in Mongolia can. They are throat singers. They can sing two, three, and even four notes at one time. They can sing high notes while singing lower notes to go with a song.

1. Mongolia is a country in Asia. What does this paragraph tell you about Mongolia?

   _____

   _____

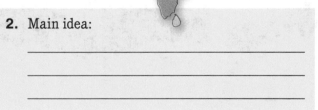

Step 2: Identify the Main Idea

Knowing the topic can help you find the **main idea,** or what the writer wants to tell you about the topic. Any summary should include the author's main idea.

Sometimes, the main idea is in the first or second sentence. Sometimes, it is in the last sentence. Find the main idea in the paragraph below.

> Throat singing has been passed down for hundreds of years in Mongolia and nearby lands. It takes strength and concentration. When throat singing began, both men and women sang. Over time it became something mostly men did. And now, it is becoming popular among women again.

2. Main idea:

   _____

   _____

   _____

Sometimes the main idea is not stated, and you have to figure it out. What is the main idea of this paragraph? How do you know?

> Mongolia was a land of nomads—people who moved from place to place. They carried everything they owned. As a result, the nomads relied on their voices for music on their travels.

3. Main idea:

   _____

   _____

Step 3: Identify Important Details

Once you have identified the topic and the main idea, look for **important details**. Details explain something or add information about the main idea. When you look for important details, ask yourself, *Does this detail help me understand the main idea? Is it important?* Focusing on only the important details will help you understand and remember what you have read.

Some people think of throat singing as a copy of nature. Singers listen to birds, to rain and thunder, to waterfalls and other natural things. They use their voices to make similar sounds. The tapping of a beetle and the murmur of a brook found their way into the songs. Singers use their voices to sound like animal cries.

4. What are important details in this paragraph?

_____

_____

_____

Step 4: Summarize

When you **summarize,** you briefly state the main idea of a paragraph or passage in your own words. You also include the important details. Think to yourself, *What would I tell a friend about what I just read?*

Below is a passage with two paragraphs. The main idea of the first paragraph is: *Throat singing is a hard skill to learn.* A good summary of this paragraph is: *Throat singers practice a lot using their tongue, lips, and teeth to make sounds.*

How do throat singers make such music? It is a hard skill to learn. Singers learn to use their voices to create quick movements, or vibrations, in their throats and mouths. They learn to use their teeth, tongues, and lips to direct the vibrations. They add clicks by placing the tongue against the teeth. They open and close their mouths to shape the sound. They practice! Only about one out of every 200 children are successful at throat singing.

For centuries, the mysterious sounds of throat singing were only heard in Mongolia and nearby nations. Today, people can go on the Internet to learn about throat singing. Many Web sites offer recordings of the songs. You can also see pictures of the singers. You can see the instruments that today's singers use to make their music even more fascinating. In a way, these singers are nomads again, traveling the world to perform their challenging art for others.

5. Read the second paragraph. Write the main idea.

_____

_____

_____

6. Write a summary of the second paragraph.

_____

_____

_____

7. Write a brief summary of the whole article (all six paragraphs) by combining all of the information you have read on these two pages.

_____

_____

_____

_____

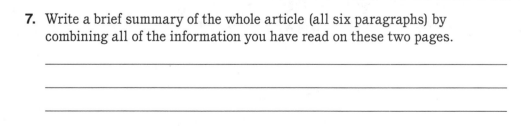

Division

Learn the SKILL

The opposite of addition is subtraction and the opposite of multiplication is division. When you divide, you separate something into equal groups. Think of a bag of 20 marbles that you need to divide into equal groups. How many different ways can you divide the marbles?

VOCABULARY

Watch for the words you are learning about.

divisible: when a number that can be divided by a whole number evenly (no remainder)

factor: a whole number that divides another whole number with a remainder of 0

SKILL	EXAMPLE	COMPLETE THE EXAMPLE
Factors are numbers that will divide equally into another number.	Every number contains at least two factors, 1 and itself. All numbers that are NOT factors of a number will NOT divide equally into that number. For example, 4 will not divide equally into 13, so 4 is not a factor of 13.	Write at least four factors of 20. _____
A number is said to be **divisible** by another number if it can be divided evenly by that number. There are a few simple tricks to see if a number is divisible.	To see if you can divide by 2, 5, or 10, use these tests: You can divide all even numbers by 2. Any number that ends in 5 or 0 is divisible by 5. Any number ending in 0 is divisible by 10.	Write a division problem using one of the rules to the left. _____
There are rules of divisibility as well for dividing by 3, 4, 6, and 9.	To see if a number is divisible by 3, add up its digits. If the sum is 3, 6, 9, or any other multiple of 3, the number itself is divisible by 3. If the digits add to 9 or a multiple of 9, then the number is divisible by 9. If an even number is divisible by 3, it is also divisible by 6. If the last two digits of a number are 00 or are divisible by 4, then the number is divisible by 4.	Write a division problem using one of the rules to the left. _____

YOUR TURN

Choose the Right Word

> division   factor   divisible

Fill in each blank with the correct word or phrase from the box.

1. The opposite of multiplication is

   _____.

2. A number is _____ by another number if it can be divided equally by that number.

3. A number that will divide equally into another number is a _____.

Yes or No?

Answer these questions and be ready to explain your answers.

4. Is 6,933 divisible by 3? _____

5. If 12 is divisible by 4, does that mean that 4 is a factor of 12? _____

6. Are all even numbers divisible by 4? _____

7. Is 2,256 divisible by 6? _____

Show That You Know

Find all the factors of the given number.

8. 20

9. 15

10. 17

11. 33

12. 47

13. 8

Determine if the following numbers are divisible by 2, 3, 4, 5, 6, 9, or 10, without actually dividing. Write the numbers in the space provided.

14. 50

15. 35

16. 124

17. 996

18. 180

SOLVE on Your Own

Skills Practice

It may help to review the divisibility rules.

**Determine if you can divide evenly.
If so, write the answer. If not, write *not divisible*.**

1. 20 ÷ 4 _____

2. 30 ÷ 6 _____

3. 18 ÷ 3 _____

4. 14 ÷ 7 _____

5. 22 ÷ 4 _____

6. 60 ÷ 9 _____

7. 177 ÷ 2 _____

8. 40 ÷ 10 _____

9. 56 ÷ 8 _____

10. 29 ÷ 2 _____

11. 34 ÷ 4 _____

12. 48 ÷ 8 _____

13. 300 ÷ 10 _____

14. 99 ÷ 9 _____

15. 87 ÷ 8 _____

16. 54 ÷ 9 _____

17. 2,124 ÷ 6 _____

18. 2 ÷ 2 _____

19. 76 ÷ 6 _____

20. 35 ÷ 7 _____

Division

Strategy

Draw a Picture or Use a Model

Step 1: Read Mr. Reed's class is visiting the art museum on a field trip. The museum has a small cafeteria where students can sit to eat their snacks. Today 24 students buy snacks. Each table in the cafeteria is filled. If the students sit in equal groups of four, how many tables are in the cafeteria?

STRATEGY	SOLUTION
Draw a Picture There are many different strategies you can use to help you with a problem like this one. One method is to draw a number line. Drawing a number line helps you understand the problem and can be a good guide to help with repeated subtraction.	Step 2: Plan Draw a number line showing 0 to 24. Use the number line to help you subtract. 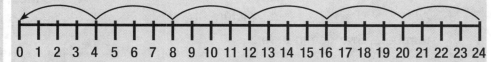 $24 - 4 - 4 - 4 - 4 - 4 - 4 = 0$ Step 3: Solve Use the number line to help you divide. Count backward by 4s (equal groups of students). How many times did you subtract four to reach zero? You counted back six times. So there must be six tables. If you are not sure of your answer, try counting back again to see if your answer is the same. It is okay if you have to count a few times to be sure. Step 4: Check Use multiplication to check your division. $4 \times 6 = 24$
Use a Model You can also use small objects, such as counters or paperclips, to model the problem. With counters, you can show arrays to help you work through the problem. Counters can help you visualize the problem. It is also easy to check your answer when using counters.	Step 2: Plan Use 24 counters. Sort them into groups of four. (Each counter represents one student.) Then count the number of groups to find the answer. 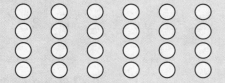 Step 3: Solve How many groups of counters are there? There are six. So there must be six tables. Step 4: Check Look over the counters to be sure there are four and only four in each group. Then count the total number of counters in your array. The total should match the number of counters you started with.

➤ YOUR TURN

Choose the Right Word

divide   number line   divisible

Fill in each blank with the correct word or phrase from the box.

1. A number is _____ by another number when it can be split into equal groups with nothing left over.

2. A _____ is a picture of numbers arranged in order.

3. To break something into groups is to _____.

Yes or No?

Answer these questions and be ready to explain your answers.

4. Can 66 ÷ 11 be solved by looking at 66 − 11 − 11 − 11 − 11 − 11 − 11? _____

5. Can a number be divided by 0? _____

6. Are there only two factors of every number? _____

7. Is two a factor of all even numbers? _____

Show That You Know

Find the answer for each problem. Use counters or draw number lines if you need to.

8. 25 ÷ 5

9. 28 ÷ 7

10. 36 ÷ 6

11. 27 ÷ 3

12. 48 ÷ 6

List the factors for each number.

13. 16

14. 24

15. 2

16. 33

17. 56

READ on Your Own

Reading Comprehension Strategy: Summarizing

Everyday Sound and Music, *pages 3–4*

Before You Read

Think about the sounds you hear every day. Which of these sounds have meaning for you? How do you separate background sounds from sounds used to communicate?

As You Read

Read "The Sounds Around You," pages 3–4.

Then fill in the chart below.

The Sounds Around You
Topic: _____
Main Ideas: _____   _____
Important Details: _____   _____   _____
Summary: _____   _____   _____   _____

VOCABULARY

Watch for the words you are learning about.

communication: the act of sharing information or feelings

eardrum: part of the ear that vibrates in response to sound waves

echolocation: a way to locate objects based on sending out sound waves and listening for echoes

pharynx: part of the throat near the vocal chords

vocal chords: parts of the body that vibrate to make the sounds of speech

windpipe: a passageway for air into the body

Fluency Tip

Search the text for new words. Practice reading them aloud so you are comfortable pronouncing them.

After You Read

Of the information in "The Sounds Around You," what did you think was the most interesting?

_____

SOLVE on Your Own

Everyday Sound and Music, *page 5*

Organize the Information

Read You Do the Math in the magazine. Then use a flowchart like the one shown below to guide you through steps of solving the problem.

Choose a simpler number to represent the song: 24

Divide the song into 6 equal parts.
24 ÷ 6 = 4

Add a zero to your answer to find out how many times the phrase is repeated during your whale song.
Phrase repetitions = 40

Multiply by 3 to find the number of long cries in the song.
40 × 3 =120

Multiply by 3 to find the number of short chirps in the song.
40 × 3 =120

Drawing a picture may help you answer the questions.

You Do the Math

Use the information from your flowchart to answer these questions. Write your answers in the space provided.

1. How did you choose the number of parts for your whale song when you were told that there are 6 repeating phrases? How did you simplify the problem and find the number of long and short sounds?

    _____

    _____

2. How many clicks, whistles, and calls would there be in a whale song with 320–360 parts if it has 6 repeating phrases of 4 clicks, 2 whistles, and 3 calls?

    _____

    _____

After You Solve

What types of patterns are there in songs that you like to sing or listen to?

_____

_____

Long Division

Learn the SKILL

Division has a language of its own in order to keep each part organized. In any division problem $a \div b = c$, the dividend is a, the divisor is b, and the quotient is c. The dividend is the number being divided. The divisor is the number you are dividing by. If the divisor goes into the dividend with nothing left over, then the divisor is a factor of the dividend. The quotient is the answer to a division problem. Since not every problem can by solved easily, knowing the parts of division will help you understand long division.

VOCABULARY

Watch for the words you are learning about.

algorithm: is a set of rules or a process for solving a problem

dividend: the number to be divided

divisor: the number to divide by

place value: the value of the place where a digit appears in a number

quotient: the answer to a division problem

SKILL	EXAMPLE	COMPLETE THE EXAMPLE
An **algorithm** is a set of rules or a process for solving a problem. The process of long division is an algorithm. With this process, you divide each digit separately.	$$\begin{array}{r} 11 \\ 4\overline{)44} \\ -4 \\ \hline 04 \\ -4 \\ \hline 0 \end{array}$$ Think of each digit as a separate number. Each number is divided.	Solve $33 \div 3$ using the algorithm for long division.
When solving division on paper, write the problem as $$\text{divisor}\overline{)\text{dividend}}^{\text{quotient}}$$ This way, you can account for the **place value** of each digit as you divide.	$$\begin{array}{r} 1 \\ 4\overline{)56} \\ -4 \\ \hline 1 \end{array}$$ The digit 5 in 56 represents 50. How many 4s go into 5? The answer is 1. $$\begin{array}{r} 1 \\ 4\overline{)56} \\ -4 \\ \hline 16 \end{array}$$ You have 1 ten left over. Add the digit 6 to the 1 ten, and you have 16 ones. $$\begin{array}{r} 14 \\ 4\overline{)56} \\ -4 \\ \hline 16 \\ -16 \\ \hline 0 \end{array}$$ Now you can finish the problem. How many 4s go into 16? The quotient is 14.	Find the quotient of $72 \div 2$ using the algorithm for long division.

YOUR TURN

Choose the Right Word

divisor   quotient   place value

Fill each blank with the correct word or phrase from the box.

1. The answer to a division problem is the _____.

2. The value of a digit in a number is determined by its _____.

3. A _____ of a number can also be a factor of that number.

Yes or No?

Answer these questions and be ready to explain your answers.

4. If you multiply a quotient by a dividend, will you get the divisor? _____

5. If you multiply a quotient by a divisor, will you get the dividend? _____

6. If a divisor is greater than 1, will the quotient be less than the dividend? _____

Show That You Know

Fill in the boxes below.

7.
```
    2
  3)8 4
  - 
      4
  - 
```

8.
```
  5)8 5
  - 
     5
  - 
```

List the factors for each number.

9. 12

10. 33

11. 42

12. 70

13. 99

SOLVE on Your Own

Skills Practice

On a separate sheet of paper, use long division to solve the problems below. Write your answer on the line.

Remember to start dividing from left to right.

1. 75 ÷ 5 _____

2. 99 ÷ 9 _____

3. 84 ÷ 7 _____

4. 74 ÷ 2 _____

5. 39 ÷ 3 _____

6. 54 ÷ 6 _____

7. 96 ÷ 8 _____

8. 92 ÷ 4 _____

9. 72 ÷ 3 _____

10. 95 ÷ 5 _____

11. 12 ÷ 2 _____

12. 35 ÷ 7 _____

13. 64 ÷ 2 _____

14. 30 ÷ 5 _____

15. 52 ÷ 2 _____

16. 63 ÷ 3 _____

17. 100 ÷ 1 _____

18. 48 ÷ 2 _____

Long Division

Strategies

Make a Table or a Chart, Draw a Picture or Use a Model

Step 1: Read The sixth grade is selling packs of handmade greeting cards for a fund-raiser. Each pack has four cards. They sell packs of 10 for $40, and individual packs for $8. If they sell 96 cards, how much money will they raise? Show all possible answers. (Hint: There are three possible answers.)

STRATEGY	SOLUTION
Make a Table or a Chart A table can organize the information in a way that makes the possible choices clear.	Step 2: Plan Calculate the number of packs that are sold. Make a table where each row corresponds to a different possible combination of 10 packs and single packs and show the money raised. Step 3: Solve Since there are 96 cards and each pack has 4 cards, the number of packs is $96 \div 4 = 24$. The possibilities are:

10 Packs	Single Packs	Money Raised
2	4	$2 \times \$40 + 4 \times \$8 = \$112$
1	14	$1 \times \$40 + 14 \times \$8 = \$152$
0	24	$0 \times \$40 + 24 \times \$8 = \$192$

Step 4: Check Use inverse operations to check the first row. If $2 \times \$40 = \$80$ and $4 \times \$8 = \$32$, then $\$80 + \$32 = \$112$. If you subtract either 80 or 32 from 112, you should get the other number: $\$112 - \$80 = \$32$. The answer checks.

Draw a Picture or Use a Model Draw a picture to help you see the problem.	Step 2: Plan Draw 24 cards as different groups of tens and ones. Then find the cost of each group. Step 3: Solve

Group 1: $2 \times \$40 + 4 \times \$8 = \$112$

Group 2: $1 \times \$40 + 14 \times \$8 = \$152$

Group 3: $0 \times \$40 + 24 \times \$8 = \$192$

Step 4: Check Use subtraction and division to check addition and multiplication. For Group 1, use $\$112 - \$32 = \$80$ to find the cost of the 10 packs. Then divide by the cost per 10 pack to find the number of 10 packs: $\$80 \div \$40 = 2$ 10 packs. The answer checks.

YOUR TURN

Choose the Right Word

```
algorithm   dividend   place value
```

Fill each blank with the correct word or phrase from the box.

1. A set of rules for solving a problem, such as using long division, is a(n) _____.

2. The place where a digit is found in a number is its _____.

3. A number divided by a divisor is a(n) _____.

Yes or No?

Answer these questions and be ready to explain your answers.

4. Can a multiple of four be divided evenly by four? _____

5. Are quotients always greater than 10? _____

6. Can a quotient be zero? _____

7. Can an algorithm use both addition and subtraction? _____

Show That You Know

List the factors for each number.

8. 49

9. 36

10. 10

11. 31

Use long division to find the quotients. Show your work.

12. $37 \div 1$

13. $45 \div 3$

14. $78 \div 6$

15. $52 \div 4$

READ on Your Own

Reading Comprehension Strategy: Summarizing

Everyday Sound and Music, *pages 6–7*

VOCABULARY

Watch for the words you are learning about.

rhythmic: following a repeated pattern

Fluency Tip

Pause before each heading in a text to set that section apart. Then read smoothly to the end of each sentence or any natural break.

Before You Read

Think back to what you read in "The Sounds Around You." What do people and animals use sounds for?

As You Read

Read "Sending Messages," pages 6–7.

Then fill in the chart below for the sections "Drums that Talk" and "Drum Codes" on page 7.

Drums That Talk	Drum Codes
Main Idea: _____ _____	**Main Idea:** _____ _____
Important Details: _____ _____ _____ _____ _____	**Important Details:** _____ _____ _____ _____ _____

After You Read

What do you use to communicate over long distances?

_____

_____

SOLVE on Your Own

Everyday Sound and Music, *page 8*

Organize the Information

Read You Do the Math in the magazine. Then use the information to finish the flowchart shown below.

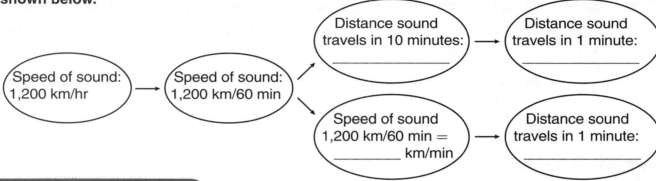

Speed of sound: 1,200 km/hr → Speed of sound: 1,200 km/60 min →

Distance sound travels in 10 minutes: _____ → Distance sound travels in 1 minute: _____

Speed of sound 1,200 km/60 min = _____ km/min → Distance sound travels in 1 minute: _____

You Do the Math

Use the information in the flowchart to answer these questions. Write your answers in the space provided.

1. Based on the flowchart, how long would it take for the sound to travel 19 km?

   _____

   _____

2. Suppose a slit gong sends a warning message at 2:00 AM. The message arrives in the nearest village at 2:01 AM. The drummer there immediately hits another slit gong and passes the message to the next village. It arrives there at 2:02 AM. This continues through six villages. The last village gets the message at 2:06 AM. How can you find the total distance the message has traveled?

   _____

   _____

After You Solve

Why do you think sound messages might be more useful than signals like lights or fire? Are sounds blocked by clouds or fog?

_____

_____

_____

Solve It!

The Four-Step Problem-Solving Plan

Step 1: Read	Step 2: Plan	Step 3: Solve	Step 4: Check
Make sure you understand what the problem is asking	Decide how you will solve the problem.	Solve the problem using your plan.	Check to make sure your answer is correct.

Read the article below. Then answer the questions.

Sight Under the Sea

Killer whales, beluga whales, and dolphins are all a type of whale called "toothed whales," or whales with teeth. Toothed whales are among some of the largest mammals on Earth. They usually swim near the ocean's surface, but they often swim at great depths too, where it can be too dark to see. So how do toothed whales see deep underwater?

Many toothed whales use echolocation to "see" in the dark. Toothed whales make high-pitched sounds near their blowhole. These sounds are sent out through the water around the whale. When the sound hits an object, it is reflected back to the whale. From these reflected sounds, the whale can tell what objects are around it and how far away they are. This is the same process bats use to "see" at night and in dark caves.

One problem with echolocation is that the speed of sound in water changes with temperature. Objects in cold water appear farther away than they really are. Whales must move around, constantly sending out sounds, to build a clear picture of their surroundings.

1. Is using sound always as good as using light?

   _____

   _____

   _____

2. The speed of sound in water is about 5,000 feet per second when the temperature is 77°F. How long would it take a whale sound to return from an object 10,000 feet away?

   _____

   _____

   _____

Read the article below. Then answer the questions.

Sonar

Without sound, speech and music would not exist. However, there are other uses for sound that you may not know about. One of the most common, and important, is sonar.

The word "sonar" comes from sound navigation and ranging. Sonar is a way of using sound to find objects that cannot be seen. With sonar, you can measure the size, distance, speed, and direction of objects though you cannot see them.

Most people think of submarines when they think of sonar. Sailors use sonar to know what is around a submarine when it is underwater. If they did not, the submarine might accidentally hit an underwater hill or a boat. But there are other uses for sonar besides helping submarines. Fishermen use sonar to find schools of fish to catch. Scientists use sonar to make maps of the ocean floor so they can study it. Doctors use sonar to see pictures of the inside of your body. They can also use sonar to see babies before they are born.

Fluency Tip

Read difficult passages out loud as if you were reading to a friend.

1. What are some common uses for sonar?

_____

_____

_____

2. Scientists are looking for a sunken ship. They sailed a total of 36 miles before finding it. They stopped three times before finding the ship, and they sailed an equal number of miles between each stop. How many miles did they sail between stops?

_____

3. A submarine watches a whale with sonar. At first, the whale was 570 yards away. Ten minutes later, the whale was 2,230 yards away. How many yards did the whale swim in that time?

_____

READ on Your Own

Reading Comprehension Strategy: Summarizing

Everyday Sound and Music, *pages 9–11*

Before You Read

How does the distance sound travels in air depend on temperature?

As You Read

Read "Sounds Batty!" pages 9–11.
Then answer the questions below.

How does a bat use echolocation to tell what an insect looks like?

_____

_____

_____

How can a bat tell how large an insect is?

_____

_____

How would a bat find a way into a cave in the dark?

_____

_____

_____

After You Read

If you could, how would you use echolocation?

_____

_____

VOCABULARY

Watch for the words you are learning about.

frequency: the number of times that something occurs

ultrasound: sound waves with a pitch too high for humans to hear

Fluency Tip

As you read and reread, pay attention to commas and periods. That will give you clues to the right way to say the words together.

SOLVE on Your Own

Everyday Sound and Music, *page 12*

Organize the Information

Use a chart like the one below to organize the information you find in the Math Project on magazine page 12.

Number of Bats	Number of Insects in One Night	Number of Insects in Four Nights
48	1,000	4,000

Math Project

Use the information in the chart to help you answer the questions. You may answer the questions on a piece of paper or in the space provided below. Remember to use the Four-Step Problem-Solving Plan.

1. Which do you think you should consider first, the total number of insects eaten or the number of bats? Why?

_____

2. How could the Try a Simpler Form of the Problem Strategy help you find factors?

_____

_____

_____

3. How many insects did the bats eat in four nights? Explain how you solved the problem.

_____

After You Solve

How could you solve the problem by using counters?

_____

_____

Dividing Multidigit Dividends

Learn the SKILL

Another way to think of division, besides splitting a number of objects into equal groups, is how many times one number can go into another number. So for 16 ÷ 4, 4 will go into 16 four times and leave no remainder (nothing left over.) Just like other mathematical operations, division can be broken down into smaller pieces, even if you are dividing with larger numbers. How would you divide 47,132 by 4?

SKILL	EXAMPLE	COMPLETE THE EXAMPLE
Place value is important for long division. It puts numbers in order and makes the work easier. It is important to know that you are only dividing each place value.	4)47,132 Each place value is divided by 4, even the hundreds place, despite the fact that a 4 cannot go into a 1. Think of how you solved a similar problem in Lesson 3.	Write a long division problem and identify the place values. _____ _____ _____ _____ _____
The long division algorithm can take longer to perform than other methods, and there can be a lot of numbers. But the work is no different from what you have done before. More steps may be involved, but you will often find yourself repeating steps.	$$\begin{array}{r} 11,783 \\ 4)\overline{47,132} \\ -\underline{4} \\ 7,132 \\ -\underline{4} \\ 3,132 \\ -\underline{2\,8} \\ 332 \\ -\underline{32} \\ 12 \\ -\underline{12} \\ 0 \end{array}$$	To show this, write 1 above the 4 in 47,132 as shown. Then multiply 1 times 4 and subtract the product from the 4 in 47,132. If you keep the numbers in columns, you will not lose track of their place value. Then you can divide 7,000 in the same way by pulling down the 7. Repeat the process until you have worked through each digit.	Solve 783 ÷ 3 with long division. _____

Choose the Right Word

> divide   factor   place value

Fill in each blank with the correct word or phrase from the box.

1. Five is a _____ of 10.

2. _____ shows the value of a digit in a number.

3. To _____ is to separate a number into equal parts or to see how many times one number goes into another number.

Yes or No?

Answer these questions and be ready to explain your answers.

4. Do you need to subtract and multiply when doing long division? _____

5. Is long division simply breaking a number down by place value? _____

6. Are all even numbers evenly divisible by two? _____

7. When you divide a number by one, will you have a remainder? _____

Show That You Know

Fill in the boxes below.

8.
```
      2 ■■
   3)888
   -■
    ■8
   -■■
     ■8
   -■■
     ■
```

9.
```
     12 ■
   7)875
   -■
    ■7
   -■■
    ■■
   -■■
     ■
```

Without dividing, write if each number is divisible by 2, 3, 4, 5, 6, 9, or 10.

10. 8,128

11. 9,999

12. 10,002

13. 100,890

14. 1,718,127

SOLVE on Your Own

Divide using long division.

In long division of a multidigit dividend, you divide and then subtract each digit.

1. 615 ÷ 5 _____

2. 936 ÷ 9 _____

3. 336 ÷ 8 _____

4. 539 ÷ 7 _____

5. 1,722 ÷ 6 _____

6. 6,912 ÷ 2 _____

7. 7,611 ÷ 3 _____

8. 4,571 ÷ 7 _____

9. 12,712 ÷ 8 _____

10. 65,515 ÷ 5 _____

11. 2,446 ÷ 2 _____

12. 95,456 ÷ 4 _____

13. 426 ÷ 3 _____

14. 212 ÷ 2 _____

15. 12,345 ÷ 5 _____

16. 1,576 ÷ 8 _____

17. 651,287 ÷ 7 _____

18. 1,203 ÷ 3 _____

Dividing Multidigit Dividends
Strategies
Try a Simpler Form of the Problem, Make a Table or a Chart

Step 1: Read A city with 30,870 citizens has an election. The city is divided into five zones with an equal number of citizens in each zone. Of the two people running for office, whoever wins the most zones wins the election. Is it possible for a candidate to win with 8,900 votes?

STRATEGY	SOLUTION
Try a Simpler Form of the Problem Use what you know to break down the problem into smaller pieces. Then make a list of what you know.	Step 2: Plan Break the problem into simple steps to solve. Find the number of voters in each zone. To win a zone, a candidate needs one more than half the votes in the zone. Multiply that number by the number of zones needed to win, and compare to 8,900 votes. Step 3: Solve 30,870 people $\div$ 5 zones = 6,174 people in each zone. To find the number of votes needed to win one zone, divide the number of people per zone by two. 6,174 people $\div$ 2 = 3,087. To win a zone, a candidate must get at least 3,087 + 1 = 3,088 votes. As there are five zones, a candidate must win greater than half the zones to win the election. Three zones is greater than half of five zones. Multiply three zones by the number of votes needed to win each zone: 3 zones $\times$ 3,088 votes = 9,264 votes 9,264 > 8,900, so the candidate cannot win with only 8,900 votes. Step 4: Check Use inverse operations to check: 9,264 $\div$ 3 = 3,088; 3,088 $-$ 1 = 3,087; 3,087 $\times$ 2 = 6,174; 6,174 $\times$ 5 = 30,870. The answer is correct.
Make a Table or a Chart Make a table or a chart to organize your information as you solve each step of the problem.	Step 2: Plan For each number of zones you want the smallest number of votes needed to win the zone, and then the number of votes needed to win the election. Write down what you know and what you need to know, and use this to fill in the table. Step 3: Solve

Number of Zones	Votes per Zone	Votes to Win Each Zone	Votes to Win
5	30,870 $\div$ 5 = 6,174	6,174 $\div$ 2 = 3,087; 3,087 + 1 = 3,088	3,088 $\times$ 3 = 9,264

9,264 > 8,900, so the candidate cannot win with only 8,900 votes.

Step 4: Check Use inverse operations to check: 9,264 $\div$ 3 = 3,088; 3,088 $-$ 1 = 3,087; 3,087 $\times$ 2 = 6,174; 6,174 $\times$ 5 = 30,870. The answer is correct.

YOUR TURN

Choose the Right Word

divide   factor   place value

Fill each blank with the correct word or phrase from the box.

1. To find how many groups there are or how much is in each group you have to _____.

2. If the numbers A and B are multiplied to find a product, A and B are _____ of the product.

3. The value of a digit based on its position is known as its _____.

Yes or No?

Answer these questions and be ready to explain your answers.

4. Can you only divide a number into equal groups if you divide a number by one of its factors? _____

5. If a number ends in zero, can it only be divided by 2, 5, or 10? _____

6. In long division is it necessary to use other operations? _____

Show That You Know

Divide.

7. 575 ÷ 5

8. 378 ÷ 3

9. 516 ÷ 4

10. 672 ÷ 8

11. 369 ÷ 9

12. 1,332 ÷ 6

13. 3,311 ÷ 7

14. 3,972 ÷ 4

15. 5,224 ÷ 8

16. 13,594 ÷ 7

READ on Your Own

Reading Comprehension Strategy: Summarizing

Everyday Sound and Music, *pages 13–14*

VOCABULARY

Watch for the words you are learning about.

decibels: units used to measure the intensity of a sound wave

migration: a mass movement of people or animals

pressure: the force exerted on an area

properties: things about a person, animal, or object that make it what it is

Fluency Tip

Look for words that might be difficult to pronounce. Check a dictionary or ask someone to help you pronounce those words.

Before You Read

Division is an operation that you can use on a daily basis. What are some ways you use division?

As You Read

Read "A Whale of a Tale" on page 13.

Fill in that part of the chart below.

Read "Did You Know?" on page 14.

Fill in that part of the chart below.

Read "Faster in Water" on page 14.

Fill in that part of the chart below.

A Whale of a Tale	Did You Know?	Faster in Water
Topic:	Topic:	Topic:
Main Idea:	Main Idea:	Main Idea:

After You Read

What are some interesting facts you learned about whales?

SOLVE on Your Own

Everyday Sound and Music, *page 15*

Organize the Information

Read You Do the Math in the magazine. Then fill in the blanks below.

Sound can travel under water at a rate of _____ meters per second. This is _____ meters per minute, which is _____ kilometers per minute. This means the sound will take _____ minutes to travel _____ kilometers and _____ minutes to travel there and back.

You Do the Math

Use the information in the paragraph above to answer these questions. Write your answers in the space provided.

> Remember to use the speed of sound in water, not the speed of sound in air.

1. How did you use larger units to simplify the problem?

   _____

   _____

   _____

2. How long will it take for the sound wave to travel from Point A to Point B and back to point A again?

   _____

3. Using mental math, how long would it take for the sound wave to travel to Point B and back to Point A, if Point A and Point B are 90 km apart?

   _____

   _____

After You Solve

When are some times you might use division on a normal day?

_____

_____

_____

Solve It!

The Four-Step Problem-Solving Plan

Step 1: Read	Step 2: Plan	Step 3: Solve	Step 4: Check
Make sure you understand what the problem is asking.	Decide how you will solve the problem.	Solve the problem using your plan.	Check to make sure your answer is correct.

Read the article below. Then answer the questions.

Seeing with Sound

Many bats and whales use echolocation in order to "see" in the dark. How does it work?

Vibrations in air or in liquid, like water, cause a sound wave. This requires energy. The wave will travel because each molecule pushes on the next molecule which in turn pushes on the next, and so on. A little energy is lost with each push, so the sound will travel until there is not enough energy left to keep going.

The speed of a wave is the product of the frequency and the wavelength. Waves with a large wavelength bend around small objects, so whales and bats use high-frequency sounds to picture small things around them. How high is the frequency? At least 20,000 Hz (hertz, or cycles per second), which is the very limit of human hearing. The bat can hear sounds up to 120,000 (WB) Hz! The dolphin uses sounds up to 150,000 (WB) Hz to travel underwater.

1. People can hear frequencies up to 20,000 Hz. Do you think a blind person could use echolocation to "see"? Why or why not?

   _____

   _____

2. A cat can hear frequencies about three times higher than a human being. About how much is that in hertz?

   _____

   _____

YOUR TURN

Read the article below. Then answer the questions.

Diagnostic Ultrasound

How do you see a baby before it is born? How do you check an artery when it is inside the body? A good answer in both cases is by an ultrasound. When it is used to look for problems, it is called a diagnostic ultrasound.

How does it work? A small, hand-held device called a transducer produces ultrasounds. These sounds are very high-pitched. A human being cannot hear them. The ultrasounds travel into your body and bounce back as an echo. The transducer receives the echo and turns it into a picture of the inside of your body. Doctors can look at these pictures to help them determine how healthy you are.

So how is an ultrasound different from an X-ray? X-rays can damage your body if you are exposed to them for a very long time. An Ultrasound is not damaging. But ultrasound pictures are not very clear and they cannot show bones very well. So a doctor may still need to take an X-ray to help you get better.

1. Sound travels in soft tissue at about 1,540 meters per second. What frequency would have a wavelength of 0.01 meters?

   _____

   _____

   _____

   _____

2. Is ultrasound a good choice for viewing bone? Why?

   _____

   _____

3. If a transducer can take 30 pictures per second, how long will it take to take 300 pictures?

   _____

   _____

Fluency Tip

Try to read smoothly and expressively, just as a storyteller or news reporter would.

READ on Your Own

Reading Comprehension Strategy: Summarizing

Everyday Sound and Music, *pages 16–18*

Before You Read

You read about the blue whale in "A Whale of a Tale." Why do whales need such loud calls for echolocation?

As You Read

Read "Damaging Decibels!" pages 16–18.

For the next questions, you need to know that every time the sound goes up by 10 dB, the pressure gets 10 times greater.

A person hums at 20 dB, but sings at 60 dB. How much louder is the singing than the humming?

_____

_____

The person now sings with an orchestra, and the dB level rises to 100. How much louder than humming is the sound now?

_____

_____

After You Read

Why do people working near planes wear special headphones to protect against loud noises?

_____

_____

_____

SOLVE on Your Own

Everyday Sound and Music, *page 19*

Organize the Information

Use a list like the one below to organize the information you find in the Math Project on magazine page 19.

Total Number of Workers with Hearing Loss = _____
Total Number Rounded to Nearest Thousand = _____
Average Number of Workers with Hearing Loss = _____
Average Number Rounded to Nearest Hundred = _____
Total Number of Workers = Average Number × Number of Cities

Math Project

Use the information in the list above to help you answer the questions. You may answer the questions on a piece of paper or in the space provided below. Remember to use the Four-Step Problem-Solving Plan.

Think about how you would solve for the number of cities.

1. Why did you first estimate the answer?

   _____

   _____

2. How many states reported if the average was 812 workers and the total reports for all groups was 20,300 workers?

   _____

3. What was the average number of workers reported by 34 states if the total number of reports was 287,504?

   _____

After You Solve

How could you express the same information from the questions in a table?

_____

_____

Put It Together

Introducing Negative Numbers

You have learned about different kinds of numbers: counting numbers, whole numbers, fractions, and decimals. These numbers can be modeled on a number line. All the numbers to the right of 0 are called positive numbers. There are also numbers to the left of 0. These numbers are called negative numbers. Positive numbers are written with or without a positive sign (+) before the number. Negative numbers are written with a negative sign (−) before the number.

For every positive number to the right of 0, there is a negative number to the left of zero. They are the same distance from zero. These numbers are called opposites. The number 5 units to the right of 0 is +5. The number 5 units to the left of 0 is −5. Zero is considered neither positive nor negative.

Look at the number line.

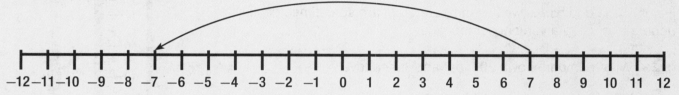

What number is the opposite of +7? The number opposite +7 is seven units to the left of 0, or −7.

What number is the opposite of −12? The number opposite −12 is 12 units to the right of 0, or +12.

Practicing Negative Numbers

Write the opposite of the given number.

1. +8 _____

2. −3 _____

3. +$\frac{1}{2}$ _____

4. What number is the opposite of 0?

_____

➤YOUR TURN ·

Thinking About Positive and Negative Numbers

Here are three examples where information is recorded in positive or negative numbers.

Temperature   Sometimes the temperature is recorded as below zero. A temperature of 4 degrees below zero can be written as −4. The thermometer here shows 20 degrees Celsius above zero.

Money   If someone owes you $5, you might think of that as +5. The person who owes you money might think of the debt as −5.

Elevation   The number of feet above sea level is given using positive numbers. Sea level is 0. Depths below sea level are indicated with negative numbers.

Heights and depths, as well as temperatures, are sometimes easier to understand using a vertical number line.

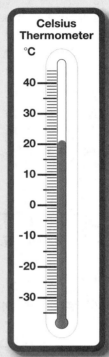

Celsius Thermometer
°C
40
30
20
10
0
-10
-20
-30

1. What number shows 200 feet above sea level? _____

2. What is the opposite of 12 degrees above zero? _____

3. Where would you find the opposite of +32 on a number line?

_____

_____

4. What number shows 10 feet below sea level? _____

5. You know that +25 is less than +30. Which negative number is less, −25 or −30? Why?

_____

Show That You Know

Read the information below, use the skills you learned to answer the questions. Use the space provided to show your work.

Dr. William Barklow of Framingham State College in Massachusetts has studied the communication between hippopotamuses. He has studied how the animal calls and hears in stereo with one channel in the air and the other in water.

In a previous lesson, you used negative numbers to indicate distance below sea level. You could also use negative numbers to indicate distance below water level or distance below ground level.

Look for key words, such as "below" and "above," to give you hints about negative and positive numbers.

1. How would you write 7 feet below water level?

2. If a hippopotamus was 15 feet below water level, how could you express its depth in the water?

3. Suppose the hippopotamus was 20 feet below water level and dove 6 more feet. How can you express its depth?

4. Which is deeper, −54 feet or −67 feet?

Show That You Know *(continued)*

5. How much deeper is —84 feet than —45 feet?

6. Find the depth at the end of each step to determine the final depth. Express each depth with the appropriate number.

   Start at water level.

   Dive 15 feet.

   Dive 8 more feet.

   Swim up 12 feet.

   Dive 20 feet.

   What is the final depth?

Review What You've Learned

7. What have you learned in this Connections lesson about how negative numbers appear on a number line?

   _____

   _____

8. What have you learned in this Connections lesson that you did not already know?

   _____

   _____

9. What have you learned in this lesson that will help you understand temperature and elevations?

   _____

   _____

Review and Practice

Skills Review

Factors:

Some **factors** for 12 are 3 and 4.

Twelve is **divisible** by 3 and by 4.

Twelve soccer balls can be divided into 3 groups that each contain 4 balls, or into 4 groups that each contain 3 balls.

Two and 6 are also **factors** for 12.

Any 12 things can be divided into 2 groups of 6 things, or 6 groups of 2 things.

All even numbers are **divisible** by 2.

Divisibility rules:

Numbers that end in 0 are **divisible** by 10; those that end in 0 or 5 are **divisible** by 5.

If the digits in a multidigit number add up to a multiple of 3, that number is **divisible** by 3; if they add up to a multiple of 9, that number is **divisible** by 9.

Even numbers that are **divisible** by 3 are also **divisible** by 6.

If the last 2 digits in a multidigit number add up to 4, that number is **divisible** by 4.

Place value in division:

$33 \div 3$ is the same as

$(30 \div 3) + (3 \div 3)$

$10 + 1 = 11$

$33 \div 3 = 11$

Long division:

$$\begin{array}{r} 16 \\ 6\overline{)96} \\ -6 \\ \hline 36 \\ -36 \\ \hline 0 \end{array}$$

Place value in division:

$3{,}321 \div 3$ is the same as

$(3{,}000 \div 3) + (300 \div 3) + (21 \div 3)$

$3{,}321 \div 3 = 1{,}000 + 100 + 7 = 1{,}107$

Long division with large dividends:

$$\begin{array}{r} 8{,}378 \\ 5\overline{)41{,}890} \\ -40 \\ \hline 18 \\ -15 \\ \hline 39 \\ -35 \\ \hline 40 \\ -40 \\ \hline 0 \end{array}$$

Strategy Review

- Use a number line to help you understand division problems.

- Set up a table or chart for division problems. Write the information you know in the chart, and fill it in with your calculations.

Skills and Strategies Practice

Complete the exercises below.

1. Is 2 a factor of 16? If so, why?

_____

2. 78 ÷ 6 = _____

3. 8,922 ÷ 3 = _____

4. 55 ÷ 5 = _____

5. List the factors of 18.

_____

6. Is 199,791 divisible by 9?

_____

TEST-TAKING tip

Prepare for a test by making a set of flash cards for divisibility rules. Write a description of a type of number on the front of each card. This could be something such as "multidigit numbers: the digits add up to a multiple of 3." On the back, write what the type of number is divisible by. In the card described, it would be "divisible by 3." Use the flash cards in a game to test your knowledge.

Mid-Unit Review

Circle the letter of the correct answer.

1. $16 \div 4 =$ _____

   A. 4   C. 6

   B. 5   D. 2

2. $123 \div 3 =$ _____

   A. 43   C. 14

   B. 41   D. 40

3. Which of these numbers is evenly divisible by 4?

   A. 109   C. 136

   B. 118   D. 225

4. $119 \div 7 =$ _____

   A. 18   C. 17

   B. 16   D. 27

5. $5,205 \div 5 =$ _____

   A. 1,040   C. 1,041

   B. 1,401   D. 141

6. Which of these numbers is divisible by 3?

   A. 412   C. 302

   B. 513   D. 200

7. $99 \div 3 =$ _____

   A. 9   C. 3

   B. 66   D. 33

8. $22 \div 2 =$ _____

   A. 11   C. 12

   B. 3   D. 4

9. $51 \div 3 =$ _____

   A. 15   C. 16

   B. 18   D. 17

10. $234 \div 6 =$ _____

   A. 37   C. 47

   B. 39   D. 36

11. Which of these numbers is divisible by both 5 and 10?

   A. 65   C. 150

   B. 115   D. 225

12. $72 \div 6 =$ _____

   A. 12   C. 13

   B. 11   D. 14

13. $90 \div 5 =$ _____

   A. 14   C. 18

   B. 15   D. 17

14. $1,004 \div 2 =$ _____

   A. 52   C. 504

   B. 520   D. 502

Mid-Unit Review

15. $36 \div 9 =$ _____

    A. 2   C. 3

    B. 27   D. 4

16. $90,000 \div 10 =$ _____

    A. 9,000   C. 90

    B. 900   D. 90,000

17. $81 \div 3 =$ _____

    A. 9   C. 27

    B. 25   D. 26

18. $176 \div 8 =$ _____

    A. 29   C. 21

    B. 20   D. 22

19. Which of the following are factors of 50?

    A. 10 and 5   C. 3 and 17

    B. 24 and 2   D. 25 and 3

20. Which of these numbers is evenly divisible by 6?

    A. 533   C. 530

    B. 528   D. 525

21. $531 \div 3 =$ _____

    A. 147   C. 177

    B. 167   D. 175

22. $56 \div 2 =$ _____

    A. 23   C. 28

    B. 27   D. 29

23. $49 \div 7 =$ _____

    A. 4   C. 6

    B. 5   D. 7

24. $171 \div 9 =$ _____

    A. 29   C. 17

    B. 19   D. 21

25. $78 \div 3 =$ _____

    A. 26   C. 36

    B. 16   D. 25

26. Which of these numbers is evenly divisible by 9?

    A. 81   C. 902

    B. 97   D. 903

27. $4,532 \div 4 =$ _____

    A. 1,032   C. 1,133

    B. 1,132   D. 1,233

28. Which of the following are factors of 48?

    A. 2 and 23   C. 24 and 5

    B. 3 and 19   D. 24 and 2

29. $16,012 \div 2 =$ _____

    A. 806   C. 7,006

    B. 8,006   D. 8,003

30. $64 \div 4 =$ _____

    A. 24   C. 16

    B. 14   D. 32

Estimation and Mental Calculation of Quotients

Learn the SKILL

In division, not all divisors will be a factor of the dividend. So sometimes it is necessary to estimate and get an answer that is close to the actual one. An estimate can also be good to check for accuracy.

VOCABULARY

Watch for the words you are learning about.

compatible numbers: numbers that are easy to compute mentally

estimate: to give an answer that is close to the correct answer

rounding: changing a number to the nearest ten, hundred, thousand, and so on

SKILL	EXAMPLE	COMPLETE THE EXAMPLE
Estimation by **rounding** is changing the dividend and/or the quotient to make it easier to solve.	You need 900 dollars to buy a new computer and you can save 32 dollars each week. How many weeks will it take you to save 900 dollars? It is harder to divide 900 by 32 than to divide 900 by 30. The answer is about 30 weeks.	Use rounding to estimate the quotient of $512 \div 5$.
Estimation by **compatible numbers** is similar to rounding but the purpose is to make the math easier to solve mentally. Typically you would round one number up and one number down to get an answer.	You need 875 dollars to buy a new computer and you can save 29 dollars each week. How many weeks will it take you to save 875 dollars? Round 29 to 30. Think about what number you could round 875 down to, in order to divide easily by 30.	Use compatible numbers to solve: $612 \div 58$.
Sometimes estimation can be used to find a range. These estimations are called overestimations and underestimations.	You need 482 dollars to buy a new computer and you can save 17 dollars each week. How many weeks will it take you to save 482 dollars? Round both numbers down and both numbers up, and record your answers. The real answer will be within this range. This is a good way to check your answer.	Use overestimation and underestimation to find a range for the quotient of $740 \div 23$.

YOUR TURN

Choose the Right Word

estimate   rounding   compatible numbers

Fill in each blank with the correct word or phrase from the box.

1. Numbers that are easy to compute mentally are called _____.

2. When _____ you change the number to the nearest ten, hundred, thousand, or so on.

3. Giving an answer that is close to the correct answer is a(n) _____.

Yes or No?

Answer these questions and be ready to explain your answers.

4. Is an estimate always the exact answer? _____

5. When using compatible numbers, if you round one number up and one number down will you always get an exact answer? _____

6. Are rounded numbers always compatible? _____

Show That You Know

For each division problem, show what you would divide to get a good estimation.

7. $124 \div 5$

8. $810 \div 13$

9. $1,067 \div 50$

10. $612 \div 19$

11. $5,392 \div 64$

12. $12,295 \div 37$

Is the answer to each division problem an overestimate or an underestimate?

13. $267 \div 10 = 30$

14. $812 \div 12 = 81$

15. $1,094 \div 18 = 55$

16. $7,512 \div 56 = 150$

17. $10,117 \div 20 = 500$

18. $90,967 \div 32 = 3,000$

SOLVE on Your Own

Skills Practice

Estimate each quotient.

Remember, compatible numbers are pairs of numbers you can divide easily.

1. 451 ÷ 83 _____

2. 7,826 ÷ 43 _____

3. 328 ÷ 17 _____

4. 1,998 ÷ 64 _____

5. 5,248 ÷ 27 _____

6. 2,300 ÷ 12 _____

7. 2,871 ÷ 69 _____

8. 9,674 ÷ 51 _____

9. 6,017 ÷ 59 _____

10. 36,512 ÷ 27 _____

11. 5,821 ÷ 5 _____

12. 8,781 ÷ 50 _____

13. 546 ÷ 5 _____

14. 75,385 ÷ 25 _____

15. 4,985 ÷ 49 _____

16. 1,250 ÷ 199 _____

Estimation and Mental Calculation of Quotients

Strategy

Try a Simpler Form of the Problem

Step 1: Read Pine Grove Pool is a rectangular pool with an area of 1,250 m². Is there enough space for 200 people to float on their backs in the pool without touching each other? (Hint: Most adults are less than 2 meters tall.)

STRATEGY	SOLUTION
Try a Simpler Form of the Problem Use what you know to solve a simpler problem. In this case, you do not need a numerical answer. You just need to know if there is enough space for 200 people. An estimate can most likely give you that answer, so you can round your numbers to make the math easier.	**Step 2: Plan** Division is the best operation to use for this problem. The dividend would be the area of the pool or 1,250 m². The divisor would be the number of people or 200. You can round 1,250 to make the problem easier. You can also divide the dividend and the divisor by 10 or 100 to make the problem even easier. **Step 3: Solve** First, you should round 1,250. You can round down to 1,200 or up to 1,300. 1,200 is easier to divide by 200, so you should round down. Remember, you do not need an exact numerical answer to solve the problem. 1,200 m² ÷ 200 people = 6 m² You can make the problem even easier by dividing both numbers by 100. As long as you divide both the dividend and the divisor by 100, it will not affect the quotient of the problem you are trying to solve. 1,200 m² ÷ 100 = 12 m² 200 people ÷ 100 = 2 people Now you have 12 m² ÷ 2 people. 12 divided by 2 equals 6. Since most adults are less than 2 meters tall, 6 m² is plenty of space for one person to float in. So the answer to the problem is yes, a pool of 1,250 m² is plenty of space for 200 people to float in. **Step 4: Check** You can use inverse operations to check your math. 2 people × 100 = 200 people 12 m² × 100 = 1,200 m² Remember that you rounded down from 1,250 at first. So your multiplication should result in the number you rounded to, 1,200.

Choose the Right Word

power of ten   estimate   mental calculation

Fill in each blank with the correct word or phrase from the box.

1. You can use _____ to solve a problem without a pencil and paper.

2. You can divide the dividend and the divisor by a(n) _____ to make a problem easier.

3. Rounding the numbers up or down can help you _____ the answer to a problem.

Yes or No?

Answer these questions and be ready to explain your answers.

4. Can you use the strategy "Draw a Picture" as a mental strategy? _____

5. If a dividend is 2,400 and the divisor is 80, can you divide the dividend by 100 and the divisor by 10? _____

6. Can you round numbers both up and down? _____

Show That You Know

Round each problem to estimate and calculate mentally. Tell why you chose those numbers.

7. $3,467 \div 732$

8. $88 \div 37$

Divide each dividend and divisor by the same power of ten and write the new problem.

9. $240,000 \div 6,000 =$

10. $180,000 \div 300 =$

11. $900 \div 450 =$

12. $32,000 \div 8,000 =$

13. $81,000 \div 900 =$

READ on Your Own

Reading Comprehension Strategy: Summarizing

Everyday Sound and Music, *pages 20–21*

Before You Read

Think about what you read in "Damaging Decibels!" What were some situations that could damage your hearing?

As You Read

Read "Sounds in Words," pages 20–21.

Complete the organizer.

Main Idea:

_____

_____

_____

Important Detail:

_____

_____

_____

Important Detail:

_____

_____

_____

Important Detail:

_____

_____

_____

After You Read

Is English a tone language? Why or why not?

_____

_____

VOCABULARY

Watch for the words you are learning about.

amplitude: a measure of the energy of a sound wave

dialects: languages that share a similar background with other languages

hertz: a unit of measure for frequency, equal to one vibration per second

larynx: the top part of the windpipe

phonation: the ability to make vocal sounds

spectrogram: a graph of the frequencies of sound

Fluency Tip

Search the text for new words. Practice reading them aloud so you are comfortable pronouncing them.

SOLVE on Your Own

Everyday Sound and Music, *page 22*

Organize the Information

Read You Do the Math in the magazine. Then complete the following table with information from the assignment.

Know	Want to Know	Learn
_____	_____	_____
_____	_____	_____
_____	_____	_____
_____	_____	_____
_____	_____	_____
_____	_____	_____

You Do the Math

Use the information in the table above to answer these questions. Write your answers in the space provided.

You will want to start by deciding how many words were learned. An even number will work better for this exercise than an odd number.

1. How many total words did you decide to have your group learn? How did you simplify the problem and find the number of people?

_____

_____

2. How many people would there be in a group that learned 250 words each of a list with 50,000 words?

_____

_____

After You Solve

Say the following words slowly: malleable, gazebo, wild, exponential. Which words "sound" best? Why? Are there any words you particularly enjoy the sound of?

_____

_____

Selecting the Most Useful Form of a Quotient

Learn the SKILL

As you have already learned, not all divisors are factors. However, since estimation does not provide an exact answer, it is necessary to find ways to show exact answers. Take, for instance, the problem 13 ÷ 5. There is only one answer for this problem but many ways to express it. How it is expressed usually depends on what a problem asks.

SKILL	EXAMPLE	COMPLETE THE EXAMPLE
A **remainder** is a whole number left over from a division problem. A remainder it is at the end of the quotient written as R and then the number.	You need to split a group of 44 people into 3 smaller, equal-sized groups. How many people will be in each group? How many people will be left over? Just divide the way you normally would. Find how many times 3 goes into 44. The people left over are the remainder. 44 ÷ 3 = 14 R2.	Divide 37 ÷ 6. Write the remainder. _____
Sometimes a remainder can be a **fraction,** a part of a whole left over.	A baker cuts a pie into 15 slices. He wants to put an equal amount of pie on four different tables. How many slices will be on each table? In this case, 4 is not a factor of 15. 15 ÷ 4 = 3 R3. But this does not explain how much pie goes on each table. In cases like this, it is important to write the answer in the form of a fraction. The remainder becomes the numerator, and the divisor is the denominator. Therefore, 15 ÷ 4 = $3\frac{3}{4}$ pieces of pie on each table.	Divide 65 ÷ 8. Show the remainder as a fraction. _____
While a fraction shows an exact number, a **decimal** is easier for purposes of place value. You know the fraction $\frac{1}{4}$ shows one part of 4, but 0.25 is often an easier number to use, especially when working with money or percents.	You bought five books for 19 dollars. If each book was the same price, what was the price per book? In this case finding a remainder or a fraction will not help, but finding a decimal amount would show the exact amount of money you spent on each book. $19 ÷ 5 = $3.80	Divide 650 ÷ 4. Turn the remainder into a decimal. _____

Choose the Right Word

remainder   fraction   decimal

Fill in each blank with the correct word or phrase word from the box.

1. A _____ is the number left over in a division problem.

2. A _____ is a good way to show part of a whole.

3. A _____ is a good way to show a remainder when you are solving problems with money.

Yes or No?

Answer these questions and be ready to explain your answers.

4. Can you show division with a fraction? _____

5. Can the remainder of a number be bigger than the divisor? _____

6. Can a decimal with a denominator of 100 be converted into a fraction? _____

Show That You Know

Write whether you would use a remainder, a fraction, a decimal, or any of the three.

7. Three friends split 13 dollars.

8. $45 \div 8$

9. A family of 4 splits 7 bottles of water.

10. A group of 5 people needs to read 97 pages.

11. A pizza is cut into a certain number of slices, and three friends share it.

Change the fraction into a decimal or the decimal into a fraction.

12. $\frac{1}{3}$

13. 0.25

14. 0.19

15. $\frac{9}{20}$

16. $\frac{7}{25}$

SOLVE on Your Own

Skills Practice

You can write a quotient with a remainder, as a mixed number, or as a decimal.

Write the quotient with a remainder as a whole number.

1. 85 ÷ 12 _____

2. 101 ÷ 11 _____

3. 1,518 ÷ 7 _____

4. 1,536 ÷ 13 _____

Write the quotient with a fraction as a remainder.

5. 109 ÷ 9 _____

6. 524 ÷ 5 _____

7. 1,698 ÷ 9 _____

8. 10,310 ÷ 15 _____

Write the quotient with a decimal remainder.

9. 315 ÷ 4 _____

10. 40,718 ÷ 8 _____

11. 6,904 ÷ 5 _____

12. 127,911 ÷ 8 _____

Selecting the Most Useful Form of a Quotient

Strategy

Draw a Picture or Use a Model

Step 1: Read Deb wants to buy some songs through the Internet. Site A sells three songs for $1.00. Site B sells four songs for $1.50. Which site should Deb buy her songs from?

STRATEGY	SOLUTION
Draw a Picture You can draw a picture based on information from the problem. Drawing pictures can help you think through problems.	Step 2: Plan Draw coins in three equal groups to find how much Site A charges per song. The coins you draw should add up to $1.00. Start by drawing a quarter in each group. Then divide the remaining quarter into nickels and pennies and draw equal amounts in each group. 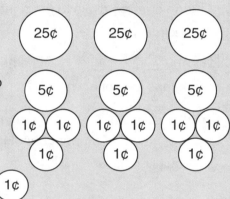 Step 3: Solve The picture shows that $1.00 divided by three is 33¢ R1 per song. But you generally do not use remainders when working with money. Instead, you should round the remainder. This gives you 33¢. So if Deb buys her songs from Site A, she will spend about 33¢ per song. Repeat steps 2 and 3 for Site B. Draw coins in four equal groups. The coins you draw should add up to $1.50. The correct drawing will show that $1.50 divided by four is 37¢ R2 per song. If you round your answer, you will have 37¢. So if Deb buys her songs from Site B, she will spend about 37¢ per song. Deb should buy her songs from Site A. Step 4: Check 37¢ × 4 = $1.48 which is close to $1.50; 33¢ × 3 = 99¢ which is close to $1.00
Use a Model You can use a model to show a problem in the same way a picture does. If you can use a model, you probably would not need to draw a picture.	Step 2: Plan You should have about 15 rods and about 30 units. Start with site A. Use 10 rods to represent $1.00. Split the rods into three equal groups. You should have one rod left over. Break the rod into 10 units and split those among the groups. You should have one single unit left over. Step 3: Solve The model shows that 100 divided into three groups is 33 with one unit left over, or $1.00 ÷ 3 = 33¢ R1. Again, you do not usually use remainders when working with money. So you can round your answer to 33¢ per song. Repeat steps 2 and 3 for Site B. Sort 15 rods into four equal groups. If you round your answer, you will find that Site B charges about 37¢ per song. Step 4: Check To check your answer, you can count all your rods and units in the groups to make sure they are the same number of cubes you started with. Do not forget to count the remainder units.

YOUR TURN

Choose the Right Word

remainder   fraction   decimal

Fill in each blank with the correct word or phrase from the box.

1. A _____ is a number with one or more digits to the right of the decimal point.

2. A _____ is a number that names part of a whole.

3. A _____ is the amount left over when a number cannot be divided equally.

Yes or No?

Answer these questions and be ready to explain your answers.

4. Can a fraction also represent a ratio or rate such as number of miles per hour? _____

5. Is 0.5 equal to $\frac{1}{2}$? _____

6. Is drawing a picture the same as using a model? _____

7. Is it best to show a remainder as a fraction when working with money? _____

Show That You Know

Change each mixed number to its decimal form.

8. $34\frac{3}{4}$

9. $9\frac{1}{8}$

10. $4\frac{2}{3}$

11. $8\frac{1}{2}$

Show each quotient as a remainder, as a fraction, and as a decimal.

12. $43 \div 5$

13. $70 \div 6$

READ on Your Own

Reading Comprehension Strategy: Summarizing

Everyday Sound and Music, *pages 23–24*

VOCABULARY

Watch for the words you are learning about.

voiceprints: tools to find out who people are by listening to their voices

Fluency Tip

Pause before each heading in a text to set that section apart. Then read smoothly to the end of each sentence or any natural break.

Before You Read

Think about the languages you read about in "Sounds in Words." What kind of language was Mandarin Chinese?

As You Read

Read "Voiceprints," pages 23–24.

Then complete the chart below. Jot down notes under the first two headings. Use complete sentences in the summary.

Main Idea:

_____

_____

Important Details:

_____

_____

_____

Summary:

_____

_____

_____

After You Read

How does it make you feel to read of high-tech imposters and identity theft?

_____

_____

SOLVE on Your Own

Everyday Sound and Music, *page 25*

Organize the Information

Read You Do the Math in the magazine. Calculate the maximum number of calls the center can receive in a month to stay within the budgeted amount. That is the amount of money the center is allowed to spend. Then fill out the following table to help you find the largest number of calls per minute that the center can take and stay in budget. Round each answer to the nearest whole number.

Maximum calls per month:	Divide by 30 days to find	Maximum calls per day:
Maximum calls per day:	Divide by 8 hours to find	Maximum calls per hour:
Maximum calls per hour:	Divide by 60 minutes to find	Maximum calls per minute:

You Do the Math

Use the information in the table above to answer these questions. Write your answers in the space provided.

> How does the information about the number of imposter calls per 1,000 help you find the total number of calls that the center can afford in a month?

1. How can you find the total number of imposter calls the budget can cover in one month? What is the total?

_____

2. Once you have the total number of imposter calls in a month, how can you find the total number of calls the center can handle in one month? What is this answer?

_____

3. What is the highest call rate per minute that the budget will allow? Show how you found your answer.

_____

_____

After You Solve

Why is it important for the center to identify the imposters?

_____

_____

Solve It!

The Four-Step Problem-Solving Plan

Step 1: Read	Step 2: Plan	Step 3: Solve	Step 4: Check
Make sure you understand what the problem is asking.	Decide how you will solve the problem.	Solve the problem using your plan.	Check to make sure your answer is correct.

Read the article below. Then answer the questions.

Numbering Systems

Throughout history, there have been many different numbering systems. Different cultures used these systems to help them count and keep track of possessions, animals, and food. Numbering systems were also important for trading.

Before 3000 B.C., the ancient Sumerians used 60 different symbols to represent 60 different numbers. The system you use has 10 symbols. The symbols are called digits: 0, 1, 2, 3, 4, 5, 6, 7, 8, and 9. You've already learned about place values. In the decimal system, 65 is 6 tens and 5 ones.

Another system is the binary numbering system. This system uses only two symbols, 0 and 1, but the place values are different from what you use. You use ones, tens, hundreds, thousands, and so on. The place values for the binary numbering system are: ones, twos, fours, eights, and so on. The binary system also works from right to left, so it may seem that you are reading the number backwards. For example, the number "1,101" means one 1, no 2s, one 4, and one 8. If you add 8 + 4 + 0 + 1, you get 13. So "1,101" is how you would write "13" in the binary numbering system.

1. Why did ancient cultures use number systems?

   _____

   _____

2. What are the 10 symbols you use to show numbers?

   _____

   _____

3. What number is equal to the binary number 110?

   _____

The **exponent** shows the number of times 10 is multiplied by 10. Here 2 is the exponent. So, $10^2 = 10 \times 10$

$$1 = \quad 1 = 10^0$$
$$10 = \quad 10 = 10^1$$
$$10 \times 10 = \quad 100 = 10^2$$
$$10 \times 10 \times 10 = \quad 1,000 = 10^3$$
$$10 \times 10 \times 10 \times 10 = \quad 10,000 = 10^4$$
$$10 \times 10 \times 10 \times 10 \times 10 = 100,000 = 10^5$$

and so on.

YOUR TURN

Read the article below. Then answer the questions.

Fan-Tan: A Division Game

In ancient times, the Chinese played a game called Fan-Tan. The game was popular in America in the 1900s. Those who played had to be good at division and determining remainders. You can play this game with three friends if you want a fun way to practice your division skills.

You will need note cards, a marker, a table, and a lot of paperclips. Write the numbers "0," "1," "2," and "3" on four separate note cards. Give a note card to each player. Then one player places a handful of paperclips on the table. Be sure you do not count them. Another player counts then divides the paperclips into four equal piles. There will be 0 to 3 paperclips left over as a remainder. Count the remainder. If the number on the player's notecard equals the remainder, that player earns one point. Keep playing and taking turns dividing until one player has five points. That player wins.

1. What skills are important in the game of Fan-Tan?

   _____

   _____

2. There are 57 paperclips on the table. What division problem would show the remainder?

   _____

3. Is it possible to have a remainder greater than 3 in Fan-Tan? Explain your answer.

   _____

   _____

   _____

Fluency Tip

Thinking through instructions as you read them can sometimes help you understand what you are reading.

READ on Your Own

Reading Comprehension Strategy: Summarizing

Everyday Sound and Music, *pages 26–28*

VOCABULARY

Watch for the words you are learning about.

chromatic scale: the 12 notes in an octave

Fluency Tip

As you read and reread, pay attention to punctuation marks that are clues to correct phrasing.

Before You Read

Think about the voiceprints you read about in "Voiceprints." Why are voiceprints a good way to identify people?

As You Read

Read "Words and Music," pages 26–28.

Then answer the questions below.

Why do scientists believe that different languages had a common basis?

_____

_____

What is the connection between speech and music?

_____

_____

Does the pattern of music change much even if the 12-note scale is not used?

_____

After You Read

There are 12 notes in the chromatic scale. Where else do you see the number 12 in your daily life?

_____

_____

SOLVE on Your Own

Organize the Information

Use a picture like the one below to organize the information you find in the Math Project on magazine page 29.

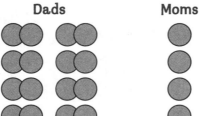

Dads   Moms

How would you draw the picture if there were only moms?

Math Project

Use the information in the picture above to help you answer the questions. You may answer the questions on a piece of paper or in the space provided below. Remember to use the Four-Step Problem-Solving Plan.

1. Which do you think you should consider first, the total number of parents or the number found by each dad and mom? Why?

   _____

   _____

2. Would it help to divide 200 by the number of parents?

   _____

   _____

   _____

3. Can you solve the problem by making each dad the same as two moms?

   _____

   _____

After You Solve

How could you express the same information in the model above as a sequence of numbers?

   _____

Writing and Solving Simple Equations

Learn the SKILL

In math, an equal sign connects two mathematical statements. It says the left side of the equation equals the right side of the equation. It is not only important to know how to solve an equation but also how to write an equation.

VOCABULARY

Watch for the words you are learning about.

equation: a mathematical sentence with an equal sign, =. An equation says that the side to the left of the equal sign has the same value as the side to the right.

inverse operations: operations that undo one another

solution of an equation: any value or values that make an equation true

SKILL	EXAMPLE	COMPLETE THE EXAMPLE
For a pan scale to be level, each side needs the same weight. An equation is similar. For an equation to be true, both sides have to be the same value. **Inverse operations** help "balance" equations.	An equation must be balanced. To find an unknown on one side, you need to balance both sides using inverse operations. Say you know $\frac{x}{5} = 20$. To solve for x, you have to use the inverse operation of division, which is multiplication. Multiply both sides of the equation by 5 to get x by itself. $$\frac{x}{5} = 20 \qquad 5 \times \frac{x}{5} = 20 \times 5$$	Use inverse operations to get x by itself. _____ _____
The point of balancing an equation is to find a **solution of an equation.** Some equations only have one solution while others can have infinite solutions. For this lesson, you will only work with equations that have one answer.	Take the equation $\frac{x}{10} = 100$. There is only one possible solution, only one possible value for x. However take the equation $\frac{x}{10} = y$. For this you simply have to find a value of x and y where the equation is true, thus there are infinite solutions.	Solve for x in $\frac{x}{5} = 11$. _____ _____
Writing an equation helps you understand what the problem means and how it can be easily solved.	Sam made \$125 mowing lawns. He was paid \$25 per lawn. How many lawns did Sam mow? For this equation, you can use either multiplication or division. Look for particular words in the question. In this case, "per" means multiplication. $$125 = 25x$$	Write a problem that can be represented with an equation. Then write the equation. _____ _____

YOUR TURN

Choose the Right Word

> equation   inverse operations
> solution of an equation

Fill in each blank with the correct word or phrase from the box.

1. A(n) _____ is an answer that satisfies an equation.

2. A(n) _____ is a mathematical sentence with an equal sign.

3. _____ are operations that undo each other.

Yes or No?

Answer these questions and be ready to explain your answers.

4. Is the number 5 an acceptable solution for x in the equation $\frac{x}{15} = 75$? _____

5. Can both sides of an equation have different variables? _____

6. Are addition and subtraction inverse operations? _____

Show That You Know

Write what you would do to both sides of the equation to find the value of x.

7. $x \div 12 = 5$

8. $2x = 3$

9. $x - 17 = 14$

10. $x \div 6 = 7$

11. $\frac{1}{4}x = 51$

Write an equation for each example below.

12. Five books cost b dollars. The total is 35 dollars.

13. Seven people shared 28 slices of pizza. Each got s slices.

14. Six people speak for m minutes during a 30-minute presentation.

15. You sold t tickets and made 516 dollars. Each ticket cost 3 dollars.

16. Each train of a roller coaster can hold 35 people. P people can ride the roller coaster in 5 trips.

SOLVE on Your Own

Skills Practice

Solve for each variable.

Use inverse operations until only the variable is on one side of the equation.

1. $a - 5 = 16$ _____

2. $b + 4 = 16$ _____

3. $12c = 108$ _____

4. $d \div 4 = 16$ _____

5. $e + 45 = 49$ _____

6. $f \div 5 = 105$ _____

7. $g \div 45 = 2$ _____

8. $16h = 152$ _____

9. $i + 4 = 22$ _____

10. $j - 4 = 2$ _____

11. $\frac{k}{5} = 50$ _____

12. $5x = 115$ _____

Solve Equations

Strategy
Make a Table or a Chart

Step 1: Read Ms. Simon works on the weekends at a flower shop. She earns $7 an hour. How much will she earn in three hours? How much in four hours? How much in seven hours? How much in nine hours?

STRATEGY	SOLUTION

Make a Table or a Chart

You can write equations to solve the problem. Then you can arrange the information in a table. A table is an easy and organized way to show all your answers at once.

Step 2: Plan Draw a table. In the top row, show the hours that Ms. Simon might work. Then for each problem, write an equation to find the amount she would earn. When you have the answer, write the amount in the table.

Step 3: Solve Write the equation $y = 3x$. The letter y represents how much money Ms. Simon earns in a weekend. The letter x represents the number of hours. You know the hours Ms. Simon might work from the problem. So you just have to replace the letter x with the right number and solve for y.

$y = 7x$
$y = 7(3)$
$y = 21$

Hours Worked (x)	3 hours	4 hours	7 hours	9 hours
Money Earned (y)	$21	$28	$49	$63

Step 4: Check Use division to check your answers.
$21 \div 7 = 3$
$28 \div 7 = 4$
$49 \div 7 = 7$
$63 \div 7 = 9$

Choose the Right Word

> inverse operations   dividend   equation

Fill in each blank with the correct word or phrase from the box.

1. In a division problem, the number you divide is called the _____.

2. Using _____ can help you solve equations.

3. In a(n) _____ , both sides of the equal sign have the same value.

Yes or No?

Answer these questions and be ready to explain your answers.

4. Can you use inverse operations to find the value of x if $32 \div x = 8$? _____

5. Is it possible for an equation to show more than one operation? _____

6. Is the answer to a division problem called the divisor? _____

Show That You Know

Use $80 \div x = y$ to find the values missing in the table. Fill in the empty spaces with the correct answers.

7.

Value of x		4		8
Value of y	40		16	

Write an equation for each situation.

8. Three plus a number is 9.

9. Six times a number is 18.

10. Five times a number plus 2 is 22.

11. Twenty minus 5 is a number.

12. Nine times a number is 27.

READ on Your Own

Reading Comprehension Strategy: Summarizing

Everyday Sound and Music, *pages 30–31*

VOCABULARY

Watch for the words you are learning about.

calypso: the traditional music of the West Indies

goombay: the traditional music and dance of the Bahamas

Fluency Tip

Remember that colons, semicolons, and commas are guides that tell you when to pause as you are reading.

Before You Read

Think about the chromatic scale you read about in "Words and Music." How is the chromatic scale related to speech?

As You Read

Read "Music of the Caribbean," pages 30–31.

Then complete the chart below. Write notes under the first two headings, and use complete sentences in the summary.

Main Idea:
Important Details:
Summary:

After You Read

How did the music of the Caribbean sustain the people who first invented it?

SOLVE on Your Own

Everyday Sound and Music, *pages 32*

Organize the Information

Read You Do the Math in the magazine. Then complete the following chart to help you set up the problem.

What number represents the whole?	Into how many equal parts is the whole divided?	How can you write that as an equation?
_____	_____	_____

You Do the Math

Use the information in the chart above to answer these questions. Write your answers in the space provided.

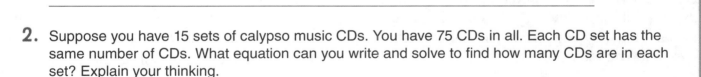

There is more than one correct way to find the answer. Which one makes the most sense to you? Explain.

1. Suppose you have 8 sets of goombay music CDs. You have 96 CDs in all.
   Each CD set has the same number of CDs. What equation can you write and solve to find how many CDs are in each set? Explain your thinking.

   _____

   _____

   _____

2. Suppose you have 15 sets of calypso music CDs. You have 75 CDs in all. Each CD set has the same number of CDs. What equation can you write and solve to find how many CDs are in each set? Explain your thinking.

   _____

   _____

After You Solve

What kind of music is your favorite? Why does that style of music appeal to you?

_____

_____

Solve It!

The Four-Step Problem-Solving Plan

Step 1: Read	Step 2: Plan	Step 3: Solve	Step 4: Check
Make sure you understand what the problem is asking.	Decide how you will solve the problem.	Solve the problem using your plan.	Check to make sure your answer is correct.

Read the article below. Then answer the questions.

Many Cultures, Many Styles

How would you build a house? You would have a few bedrooms, a kitchen, and so on. But if you look throughout the United States, you will find many different styles of houses.

The earliest settlers from Europe built houses that were similar to what they knew. There were different styles for the Spanish, French, and English settlers. The differences were not only in their shapes but also in the materials they used. Later, the settlers started developing their own styles.

Just as there were Spanish, French, and English styles, other countries had styles too. Grecian (Greek) style had many columns and was very popular. Many churches in Europe were built in the Gothic style, with pointed arches and many windows.

Some modern examples from the United States include Pueblo and Prairie styles. There are also modern European and Near Eastern styles. Sometimes a style is based on function, while other times it is based on appearance.

1. What are some features of the Gothic style?

   _____

   _____

   _____

2. Mr. Stamos designs a large hall with 22 Greek-style columns. He has one column for every 12 square feet of floor space. What equations would show the floor's total number of square feet? Write at least two equations. Include a variable in each equation.

   _____

   _____

   _____

YOUR TURN

Read the article below. Then answer the questions.

Frank Lloyd Wright

Frank Lloyd Wright was America's most famous architect. Born in 1867, he studied engineering in college because there was no course in architecture. He spent six years as an apprentice before working on his own.

Wright developed a style of house called Prairie. These houses had low horizontal lines and open interior spaces because he felt that the common architecture was boxy and confining. He divided rooms by glass panels instead of walls. He wanted his houses to blend in with the flat Midwest prairie.

Wright was concerned about common people. During the Great Depression he developed a low-cost version of the Prairie style called Usonian. These houses had no basements or attics and were built on slabs.

Another of his styles was called hemicycle, because it featured half circles. An example of this is the Guggenheim Museum.

Fluency Tip
Take your time when reading complex material so you can make sense of difficult ideas.

1. Suppose it costs $200,000 to build a house which has an area of 2,500 square feet. What is the cost per square foot?

_____

_____

2. If the cost of building a basement is twice as much as the cost of building the first floor, what does it cost to build a basement if the first floor costs $30,000?

_____

3. Each floor can be built in $\frac{1}{3}$ the time it takes to build a basement. How many floors would there be if the basement takes half the building time?

_____

_____

_____

READ on Your Own

Reading Comprehension Strategy: Summarizing

Everyday Sound and Music, *pages 33–35*

VOCABULARY

Watch for the words you are learning about.

corrido: a traditional type of music from Mexico

Fluency Tip

As you read and reread, pay attention to punctuation marks that are clues to correct phrasing.

Before You Read

Think about the music of the West Indies that you read about in "Music of the Caribbean." How did calypso music get started?

As You Read

Read "Music of Mexico," pages 33–35.

Then answer the questions below.

What is a corrido, and what does its rhythm tell you?

_____

_____

Which European dances influenced Tejano music?

_____

_____

How would an African instrument become popular in Mexico?

_____

_____

After You Read

Can you think of any new musical styles that are based on older musical styles?

_____

_____

SOLVE on Your Own

Everyday Sound and Music, *page 36*

Organize the Information

Make a table like the one below to help you solve the problem in the Math Project on magazine page 36.

Name	Relationship
Anthony	Carmen × 2
Carmen	Mario + 6
Mario	$\frac{1}{2}$ Juan
Juan	28 hours

Start by plugging in the information you know.

Math Project

Use the information in the table to help you answer the questions. You may answer the questions on a piece of paper or in the space provided below. Remember to use the Four-Step Problem-Solving Plan.

1. Write and solve an equation to find how many hours each person works in a week.

_____

_____

_____

_____

2. How many hours would Anthony work if Juan worked 10 hours each week? Show your work.

_____

_____

_____

After You Solve

How could you solve the problem using a diagram?

_____

_____

Put It Together

Order of Operations

You have learned how to add, subtract, multiply, and divide whole numbers. When a problem involves just one operation, you know how to calculate the answer. What happens if there are several operations in one problem? Mathematicians have established an order of operations to make sure everyone gets the same answer. Without these rules there could be different results. Only one answer is correct.

1. Do the work in parentheses first.

    $19 - (10 + 3) = $ _____

    (add 10 + 3 first)

    $19 - 13 = 6$

2. Multiply and divide from left to right. As you move from left to right do whichever multiplication or division comes first.

    $3 \times 10 - 8 \div 2 = 30 - 4 = 26$

    $15 \div 3 \times 6 = 5 \times 6 = 30$

3. Add and subtract from left to right. As you move from left to right do whichever addition or subtraction comes first.

    $17 - 6 + 42 = 53$ (from left to right subtraction come first in this example)

    $16 + 45 - 23 = 38$ (from left to right addition comes first in this example)

Practicing Order of Operations

Use the order of operations to simplify these expressions.

1. $25 + (3 \times 9)$ _____

2. $16 \div 2 + 14$ _____

3. $36 - 4 \times 7$ _____

4. $6 \times 7 + 12 \div 4$ _____

Thinking About Order of Operations

Answer the questions to simplify the expression below. Use the list to help you.

$15 + 12 \div 3 \times 4 - 8$

Order of Operations

Parentheses

Multiplication and **D**ivision from left to right

Addition and **S**ubtraction from left to right

1. How many parentheses are in the expression? _____

2. Which operation should you perform first in the expression?

_____

3. What operation should you perform next in the expression?

_____

4. What operation should you perform next in the expression?

_____

5. What operation should you perform next in the expression?

_____

6. What is the value of the expression? _____

7. Simplify: $(4 + 11) \times 3 + 5 \times (8 - 2)$ _____

8. If there is more than one operation inside a set of parentheses, how do you know which operation you should perform first?

_____

9. Simplify: $(5 \times 3 + 7 - 2) + (12 + 6 \div 2)$ _____

10. If there is a set of parentheses within a set of parentheses, which should you simplify first?

_____

11. Simplify: $84 - (3 \times (4 + 8 \times 2))$ _____

Show That You Know

Read the information below, and use the skills you have learned to answer the questions. Use the space provided to show your work.

Most music has a structure. For musicians to work together in an orchestra or band, everyone must agree on and obey a set of rules. These rules include the pitch of a note, the rhythm, and the intensity of the sounds.

Mathematicians also have a structure. That structure is the order of operations.

Mary, Grace, Chloe, and Meg are trying to simplify the mathematical expression shown.

$$20 + 8 \div 4 + 3 \times 2$$

Mary thinks the answer is 20. Grace is sure the answer is 28. Chloe is positive the answer is 50. Meg says the answer is 8. Only one of the girls is correct.

Use the Order of Operations on page 91 to help you answer the questions.

1. Is Meg correct? If Meg is wrong, explain her error.

2. Is Grace correct? If Grace is wrong, explain her error.

3. Is Chloe correct? If Chloe is wrong, explain her error.

Show That You Know (continued)

4. Is Mary correct? If Mary is wrong, explain her error.

5. Simplify this expression: $(4 + 11 \times 7) \div (12 - (5 - 2))$. Explain how you simplified the expression.

6. Write your own expression that contains parentheses, addition, subtraction, multiplication, and division. Explain how the expression should be simplified.

Review What You've Learned

7. What have you learned in this Connections lesson about how to use the order of operations?

Review and Practice

Skills Review

Estimating quotients:

Round dividends or divisors to estimate quotients.
$400 \div 43 \rightarrow 400 \div 40 = 10$.
$\frac{400}{43}$ is approximately equal to 10.

Use **compatible numbers** to estimate quotients.
$203 \div 52 \rightarrow 200 \div 50 = 4$.
$\frac{203}{52}$ is approximately equal to 4.

Estimating a range of quotients:

Round the dividend and divisor to make an overestimation and an underestimation of a quotient. The actual quotient should be between these two numbers. For $616 \div 17$:

$600 \div 15 = 40$ (overestimate)

$620 \div 20 = 31$ (underestimate)

$616 \div 17$ is between 31 and 40.

Remainders and fractions:

$53 \div 2 = 26 \text{ R } 1$

$$
\begin{array}{r}
26 \\
2\overline{)53} \\
-4 \\
\hline
13 \\
-12 \\
\hline
\text{R}1
\end{array}
$$

Or: $53 \div 2 = 26 \frac{1}{2}$; the remainder is shown as a fraction of the divisor.

Quotients with decimals:

Sometimes it is best to show a quotient as a decimal. This is the case with money.

$\$49 \div 4 = \$12 \frac{1}{4}$

$\frac{1}{4}$ is the same as 0.25

$\$49 \div 4 = \$12.25$

Writing equations:

Danette had 4 banana slices, and her sister gave her x more. She then had 13 slices.

$4 + x = 13$

x is an unknown. In this case, it represents the slices Danette's sister gave to her.

Solving equations:

Use **inverse operations** to find the value of an unknown, or the **solution of an equation.**

$4 + x = 13$

$4 + x - 4 = 13 - 4$

$x = 9$

Strategy Review

- Use a table to show multiple answers in an organized way.

- Use inverse operations to help solve division equations.

Skills and Strategies Practice

Solve the exercises below.

1. Use compatible numbers to estimate the quotient for $504 \div 11$.

_____

_____

2. What is the value of c?
$12c = 24$

_____

3. Write the quotient for $74 \div 5$ as a remainder, fraction, and decimal.

_____

4. Divide the dividend and the divisor by the same power of ten, then write the new problem.
$350,000 \div 500$

_____

_____

5. What is the range of possible answers for the quotient of $745 \div 11$?

_____

_____

_____

6. Find the value of s in:
$14s = 280$

_____

TEST-TAKING tip

Be sure you understand what a test question is asking. Read it twice if necessary. Remember that when you are asked to estimate the quotient in a division problem, you are not being asked to find the exact quotient. The exact quotient may not be listed in the answer choices.

Unit Review

Circle the letter of the correct answer.

1. What is a reasonable estimate for $572 \div 5$?

    A. 115   C. 125
    B. 1250   D. 100

2. What is the quotient for $158 \div 7$ shown with a remainder?

    A. 20 R4   C. 22.4
    B. 22 R4   D. 21 R4

3. Sylvie had 16 books. She received b books from her friend. Now she has a total of 27 books. Which equation represents this situation?

    A. $16 + 27 = b$ C. $16 - 27 = b$
    B. $27 + b = 16$ D. $16 + b = 27$

4. What is a reasonable estimate for $258 \div 13$?

    A. 35   C. 10
    B. 15   D. 20

5. Which of the following would be done to solve the equation $3x = 230$?

    A. divide each side of the equation by x
    B. multiply each side of the equation by x
    C. divide each side of the equation by 3
    D. multiply each side of the equation by 230

6. What is the quotient of $2,213 \div 20$ shown with a fraction as a remainder?

    A. $100 \frac{13}{20}$ C. $110 \frac{3}{5}$
    B. $110 \frac{13}{20}$ D. $120 \frac{13}{20}$

7. What is the best way to find an estimate for $20,197 \div 41$?

    A. change to $20,200 \div 40$
    B. change to $20,200 \div 45$
    C. change to $20,100 \div 40$
    D. change to $20,100 \div 45$

8. Sarah divides $15 equally among 6 friends. How much does each friend receive?

    A. $1.50   C. $2.50
    B. $2.00   D. $3.00

9. What should be done to solve for d?
   $d - 5,709 = 23,980$?

    A. add 23,980 to each side of the equation
    B. add 5,709 to each side of the equation
    C. add d to each side of the equation
    D. subtract 5,709 from each side

10. What is a good estimate for $1,398 \div 19$?

    A. 50   C. 80
    B. 60   D. 70

11. $c \div 22 = 12$
    What can be done to solve for c?

    A. multiply each side of the equation by c
    B. multiply each side of the equation by 22
    C. subtract 22 from each side
    D. divide each side by 12

12. What is the value of c in $c \div 20 = 6$?

    A. 120   C. $\frac{6}{20}$
    B. 0.3   D. 26

13. What is the best estimate for $709 \div 70$?

    A. 99   C. 10

    B. 7   D. 15

14. Anton has 16 slices of pie. If he divides the pieces equally among 15 friends, how many slices will he have left over?

    A. 2   C. 1

    B. 3   D. 4

15. What is the quotient of $363 \div 17$ with a remainder?

    A. 22 R6   C. 20 R6

    B. 21 R7   D. 21 R6

16. How can the quotient of $3,007 \div 30$ be best estimated?

    A. by rounding 30 to 37, then dividing

    B. by rounding 3,007 to 3,000, then dividing

    C. by rounding 3,007 to 3,200, then dividing

    D. by rounding 30 to 35, then dividing

17. $h \div 4 = 200$

    $h =$ _____

    A. 800   C. 50

    B. 900   D. 500

18. $y - 35 = 5,198$

    $y =$ _____

    A. $5,198 - 35$ C. $5,198 + 35$

    B. $\dfrac{5,198}{35}$ D. $5,198 \times 35$

19. What is a reasonable estimate for $5622 \div 79$?

    A. 80   C. 70

    B. 85   D. 90

20. $6g = 720$

    $g =$ _____

    A. 120   C. 12

    B. 140   D. 130

21. $\$17 \div 5 =$ _____

    A. $3.25   C. $3.50

    B. $3.75   D. $3.40

22. Estimate the quotient of $99 \div 24$.

    A. 3   C. 5

    B. 4   D. 2

23. $\$275 \div 4 =$ _____

    A. $68.25   C. $67.75

    B. $68.75   D. $66.75

24. What is a reasonable estimate for $123 \div 11$?

    A. 10   C. 11

    B. 18   D. 15

25. $\dfrac{g}{57} = 12$

    $g =$ _____

    A. 684   C. 4.75

    B. 627   D. 475

26. What is the quotient of $1,702 \div 3$ with a fractional remainder?

    A. $467\frac{1}{3}$ C. $576\frac{1}{3}$

    B. $567\frac{1}{2}$ D. $567\frac{1}{3}$

27. $z + 35 = 39$

    $z =$ _____

    A. 7   C. 2

    B. 4   D. 3

Unit 2 Reflection

MATH SKILLS

The easiest part about estimating quotients is

The models and pictures are useful because

MATH STRATEGIES & CONNECTIONS

For me, the math strategies that work the best are

The order of operations is useful because

Everyday Sound and Music

READING STRATEGIES & COMPREHENSION

The easiest part about summarizing is

One way that summarizing helps me with reading is

The vocabulary words I had trouble with are

INDEPENDENT READING

My favorite part of <u>Everyday Sound and Music</u> is

I read most fluently when

UNIT 3
Adding and Subtracting Fractions and Decimals

MATH SKILLS & STRATEGIES
After you learn the basic **SKILLS**, the real test is knowing when to use each **STRATEGY.**

AMP LINK MAGAZINE
You Do the Math and Math Projects: After you read each magazine article, apply what you know in real-world problems. Fluency: Make your reading smooth and accurate, one tip at a time.

READING STRATEGY
Learn why **Questioning** helps you understand what you read.

CONNECTIONS
You own the math when you make your own connections.

VOCABULARY
MATH WORDS:
Know them!
Use them!
Learn all about them!

Reading Comprehension Strategy: Questioning

How to Question

Goal Setting	Question Words	Between the Lines	Beyond the Text
Ask, *What is my reason for reading this text?*	Ask, *What important details can I find in the text?*	Ask, *What decisions can I make about the facts and details in the text?*	Ask, *What connections can I make between the text and my life?*

Asking questions helps you get the most out of what you are reading. Questions such as *What do I think this article is about?* and *What will I learn?* will help you set a goal before you read. Once you have set that goal, you are more likely to remember and understand what you read. Look quickly at the text. Scan for titles, headings, pictures, captions, and boldfaced words. Ask a goal-setting question.

Smartphones and Powerusers

Many people are starting to use new cell phones called "smartphones." These phones are different from regular cell phones due to their ability to perform everyday computer functions along with regular phone functions. In addition to calling and texting, smartphones can check and send e-mail, browse the Internet, take pictures, and keep organized calendars.

1. What clues will help you ask a good goal-setting question?

_____

_____

_____

_____

Check as you read to make sure the text is answering your question. You may have to change the question.

Smartphones generally have additional hardware that makes them much easier to use than traditional cell phones. Many smartphones include a full keyboard for typing. Several smartphones also include touch sensitive screens. These features allow people to use their phones as if they were using a computer.

2. Was your goal-setting question answered?

_____

If you need to change it, ask the new question now.

_____

Asking questions about the details helps you remember what you are reading. When reading about people, ask *"Who?"* If something important happened, ask *"What?", "Where?", "When?", "Why?",* and *"How?"*

Many people have become powerusers, combining new internet and cell phone technologies. For instance, a poweruser might use a smartphone's built-in camera to take a picture and attach the picture to an e-mail.

3. What questions are answered by details in the passage?

_____

_____

_____

While reading, you may think of a question to ask. Using sticky notes can help. Write your question on one and then stick it on the page where you will find the answer. Then you can go back and review all of them after reading the article.

Another poweruser technique is to assign shortcut keys. Do you text a particular person daily? On many smartphones, you can assign a shortcut key, such as the letter T, to that person's number. When you hold down the shortcut key, the phone will automatically start a blank text ready to be sent directly to that person.

4. Write two questions you might ask yourself while reading this passage. Then, underline the answers in the text.

_____

_____

_____

Sometimes, you may not find the answer to a question in the text. Instead, you have to think about what you are reading. Why did the author include that information? What is the author trying to say? This kind of questioning is called "reading between-the-lines." How can you decide on good "between-the-lines" questions? You put together information found in different places in the text. Then put this information together with what you already know about the topic.

Cell phone technology is constantly and rapidly evolving. Some of the newest smartphones include an internal GPS for mapping and directions, wi-fi to access the Internet directly, and higher quality cameras that will take great pictures and record video.

Cell phone makers are also learning how to pack all of these features into smaller and more lightweight phones. One day soon, it's not unlikely that you'll have a wristwatch phone, or a small earpiece phone that can do everything today's phones do and more!

5. In what two places does the author describe how powerusers interact with their smartphones?

_____

_____

_____

6. Write a between-the-lines question.

_____

_____

7. What do you know about smartphones? How might that help you answer a between-the-lines question?

_____

_____

8. What text information helped you answer the between-the-lines question?

_____

_____

9. What have you learned about questioning that was the most useful?

_____

10. What have you learned about questioning that you still do not understand?

_____

Use the Strategies

Use the reading comprehension strategies you have learned to answer questions about the article below.

Code Talkers

Have you ever needed to keep your messages secret? If so, you may be familiar with codes. A code is a language of symbols, numbers, letters, or words used to communicate top-secret messages. For those who do not know the secret language, codes can be impossible to solve. Some codes are created through mathematical calculations. However, one of the most baffling secret codes of all time was already a language—Navajo.

During World War II, the U.S. Marines needed an unbreakable code to ensure success against the Japanese Imperial Army. Philip Johnston was a retired soldier who had lived with the Navajos in the American southwest. He had heard of other American Indian languages used for code during World War I. He knew that Navajo was a complex language spoken by very few non-Navajos, so he suggested using it for the new code. Soon, Navajos were recruited to work as code transmitters, or "code talkers."

They could translate three lines of English into Navajo, send the message, and interpret it back into English in 20 seconds. Simple code machines took half an hour to do this amount of work.

The code talkers' speed and accuracy is even more amazing when you think of the complexity of their code. Instead of just translating whole sentences from English to Navajo, they used a code within their language. Even if the Japanese army had been able to understand the Navajo words, the messages would not have made sense.

With the code talkers' help, the Marines exchanged important messages about troops, strategies, and orders. Their hard work saved lives and helped win battles.

1. Why did the Marines need an unbreakable code?

_____

_____

_____

_____

2. Ask and answer a "between-the-lines" question about the Navajos.

_____

_____

_____

_____

3. What are three features of the Navajo code that made it so successful in World War II?

_____

_____

_____

4. How did the Marines come to use the Navajo language as its secret code?

_____

_____

_____

_____

_____

_____

_____

Reading Comprehension Strategies: Summarizing, Questioning

Use the reading comprehension strategies you have learned in this and the previous units to answer the questions below.

1. How did the code talkers send and receive messages?

2. Why do you think American Indian languages would make successful codes?

3. Write one question that you would like to ask a Navajo code talker.

4. Because the code talkers used a "code within a code," the messages would not have made sense even to fellow Navajo-speakers. What does this tell you about the nature of understanding messages?

Problem-Solving Strategies: Draw a Picture or Use a Model, Find a Pattern

Use these problem-solving strategies to answer the questions below.

5. Harold transmits six lines of code in $\frac{2}{3}$ of a minute. Sam transmits 12 lines of code in $1\frac{1}{3}$ minutes. How many minutes did it take for all the code to be sent? Draw a picture to solve.

6. Two code talkers transmit three lines of code in 20 seconds. A machine needs half an hour to do the same. How many lines of code can the code talkers transmit in the amount of time it takes one machine to send three lines? Break the problem into simpler steps to solve. Remember that half an hour is 30 minutes, and there are 60 seconds in each minute.

Prime and Composite Numbers

Learn the SKILL

Laurie is trying to solve a puzzle. She is told that there are two composite numbers. Each number has three as a factor and a least common multiple of 48. What could the two numbers be?

SKILL	EXAMPLE	COMPLETE THE EXAMPLE
A **factor** is a whole number that can be evenly divided into another whole number. A multiple is the product of a number and a whole number.	What are the factors of 4? 1, 2, and 4 all divide evenly into 4. Is 6 a multiple of 2? Yes, because $2 \times 3 = 6$.	What are the factors of 6? _____ Is 17 a multiple of 7? _____
A **composite number** is a number that has three or more factors. A **prime number** is a number with only two factors (one and the number itself).	Is 14 a prime or a composite number? 14 is a composite number, as it has three or more factors; 1, 2, 7, and 14.	Is 16 a prime or composite number? _____
A common factor is a factor that two numbers share. The greatest common factor is the highest factor the numbers share. A common multiple is a multiple that two numbers share. The least common multiple is the smallest multiple that two numbers share.	What is the greatest common factor of 12 and 8? The greatest common factor is 4. What is the least common multiple of 4 and 10? The answer would be 20 because $4 \times 5 = 20$ and $2 \times 10 = 20$.	What is the greatest common factor of 2 and 4? _____ What is the least common multiple of 2 and 4? _____

▶YOUR TURN

Choose the Right Word

```
composite number   factor
prime number   multiple
```

Fill in each blank with the correct word or phrase from the box.

1. A _____ is the product of two numbers.

2. A _____ has only two factors.

3. A _____ has at least three factors.

4. When dividing a _____ into a whole number the remainder is zero.

Yes or No?

Answer these questions and be ready to explain your answers.

5. Can a number be both a factor and a multiple? _____

6. Can a number be both composite and prime? _____

7. Are all odd numbers prime numbers? _____

8. Can an even number be a prime number? _____

Show That You Know

Write out the factors.

9. 5

10. 8

11. 9

Write yes or no.

12. Is 6 a multiple of 48?

13. Is 12 a multiple of 6?

Write the greatest common factor.

14. 12 and 4

15. 24 and 16

Write the least common multiple.

16. 13 and 1

17. 25 and 4

SOLVE on Your Own

With even numbers you can always start with 2 as a factor.

Write out the factors.

1. 10 _____

2. 24 _____

3. 15 _____

4. 36 _____

5. 25 _____

Is the number prime or composite?

11. 15 _____

12. 11 _____

13. 14 _____

14. 2 _____

15. 21 _____

Is the number a multiple of 6? Write yes or no.

6. 3 _____

7. 12 _____

8. 48 _____

9. 100 _____

10. 1 _____

Find the greatest common factor (GCF) and the least common multiple (LCM).

16. 4 and 16 _____

17. 6 and 10 _____

18. 3 and 21 _____

19. 12 and 16 _____

20. 15 and 50 _____

Prime and Composite Numbers
Strategies
Make a List or Find a Pattern

Step 1: Read Christina is baking two kinds of bread. One recipe calls for 12 cups of flour, and the other calls for 8 cups of flour. What size measurement cups can she use for both batches?

STRATEGY	SOLUTION
Make a List Making a list can help you see which numbers match. It is easy to spot common factors or common multiples of numbers when you compare lists of the numbers' factors or multiples.	Step 2: Plan Make a list of all of the factors of 12. Under it, make a list of all the factors of 8. Circle the numbers that match. Step 3: Solve The factors of 12 and 8 are: 12 ①②, 3,④ 6, 12 8 ①②④ 8 So, 1-, 2-, and 4-cup measures can all be used. Step 4: Check Use division to check. 1, 2, and 4 all evenly divide into both 8 and 12.
Find a Pattern Finding a pattern can guide you to find the right answer.	Step 2: Plan Find a pattern for the divisors of 8 and 12. Step 3: Solve Each recipe calls for a whole number of cups of flour. Since 1 is always a factor of any whole number, a 1-cup measure will work. 12 and 8 are both even, so a 2-cup measure works as well. The results of dividing both 12 and 8 by 2 are even, so 2 can be factored into both 12 and 8 twice. Therefore, 4 is a divisor for both 12 and 8. However, dividing 12 and 8 by 4 results in two different primes, so there are no more common divisors. Step 4: Check Find common multiples of 1, 2, and 4 to check: 8 and 12 are both multiples of all three numbers.

YOUR TURN

Choose the Right Word

> factor   prime   composite

Fill in each blank with the correct word or phrase from the box.

1. A number that has only one and itself as factors is a _____ number.

2. A number that divides evenly into another number is a _____ of that number.

3. A number that has more than itself and one as factors is a _____ number.

Yes or No?

Answer these questions and be ready to explain your answers.

4. Is two the only even prime number? _____

5. Do composite numbers have more than two factors? _____

6. Is a factor of a number always smaller than that number? _____

7. Is a multiple of a number usually greater than that number? _____

Show That You Know

Find the factors of these numbers. State if the number is prime or composite.

8. 18

9. 14

10. 11

11. 27

Find the first four multiples of these numbers.

12. 3

13. 5

14. 10

15. Find the common factors of 14 and 28.

| **14** | 1, 2, 7, 14 |
| **28** | 1, 2, 7, 14, 28 |

16. Find a common multiple of 3 and 5.

| **3** | 3, 6, 9, 12, 15 |
| **5** | 5, 10, 15, 20, 25 |

READ on Your Own

Reading Comprehension Strategy: Questioning

Communication and Technology, *pages 3–4*

Before You Read

In what ways do pets or other animals communicate with humans?

As You Read

Preview the pictures and captions of "Communicating with Koko,"

pages 3–4. STOP

Write a goal-setting question in the chart below.

Then read "Communicating with Koko," pages 3–4.

VOCABULARY

Watch for the words you are learning about.

colony: a large group of animals of the same type that live together

communicate: to give and receive information

gorilla: a large member of the ape family

sign language: a language that does not use speech

Fluency Tip

Identify words that you do not know. Find out how to pronounce them before reading.

Before You Read	After You Read
Goal-setting question:	
Details question:	

After You Read

Do you think other animals can learn sign language? Explain.

SOLVE on Your Own

Communication and Technology, *page 5*

Organize the Information

To find the prime factors of your age, put your age in the top box. Then find the factors of that number. Only fill in boxes until you have prime numbers. (You may not use all of the boxes.) Do the same for Koko's age.

Your Age	Koko's Age

You Do the Math

Use the information in the table above to answer these questions. Write your answers in the space provided.

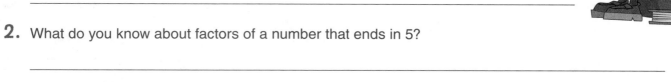

Start by subtracting to find Koko's age.

1. How can you find two factors of your number if you find that 3 or 2 is a factor?

_____

2. What do you know about factors of a number that ends in 5?

_____

3. What do you know about factors of a number that ends in 0?

_____

After You Solve

How can you train a pet to communicate with you?

_____

_____

Adding and Subtracting Fractions with Like Denominators

Learn the SKILL

Billy and Jamal are teammates on the math team. At the start of each round, they get eight questions to answer. Billy answers three of the questions correctly. Jamal answers five of the questions correctly. What fraction of the questions did they each answer correctly? How many more did Jamal answer correctly?

VOCABULARY

Watch for the words you are learning about.

simplify: to re-write in an equivalent form that represents the simplest possible value

SKILL	EXAMPLE	COMPLETE THE EXAMPLE
When adding fractions with the same denominator, add only the numerators. Keep the same denominator for the sum as you had for the addends.	Add $\frac{3}{8} + \frac{5}{8}$. Add the numerators: $3 + 5 = 8$ $\frac{3}{8} + \frac{5}{8} = \frac{8}{8}$ The denominator stays the same.	Add $\frac{2}{3} + \frac{1}{3}$. _____
Subtracting fractions with the same denominator is just like adding except the numerators are subtracted. The denominators still stay the same.	Subtract $\frac{5}{8} - \frac{3}{8}$. Subtract the numerators: $5 - 3 = 2$ $\frac{5}{8} - \frac{3}{8} = \frac{2}{8}$ The denominator stays the same.	Subtract $\frac{2}{3} - \frac{1}{3}$. _____
After adding or subtracting, **simplify** the result if necessary.	Simplify $\frac{8}{8}$ and $\frac{2}{8}$. $\frac{8}{8} = 1$ $\frac{2}{8} = \frac{1}{4}$	Simplify $\frac{3}{3}$. _____
A number line is a model that can be used to add or subtract fractions. The number line can show the fractions as parts of a whole. Count to add the parts.	Add $\frac{5}{8} + \frac{2}{8}$. Show $\frac{5}{8}$ on the number line. Then add two more eighths. A number line, such as the one below, can be used to find $\frac{5}{8} + \frac{2}{8} = \frac{7}{8}$. 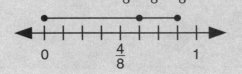	Use a number line to add two fractions with the same denominator.

YOUR TURN

Choose the Right Word

> add   subtract   fraction   simplify

Fill in each blank with the correct word or phrase from the box.

1. To _____ is to find the total.

2. A(n) _____ shows part of a whole.

3. To _____ means to take a part away.

4. To _____ is to replace an expression with its simplest form.

Yes or No?

Answer these questions and be ready to explain your answers.

5. Is it possible to add two fractions? _____

6. If two fractions have the same denominator, will the difference between them have a different denominator? _____

7. Is it possible for the total of two fractions to equal one? _____

Show That You Know

Add or subtract the fractions. Simplify if possible.

8. $\frac{5}{6} + \frac{1}{6} =$

9. $\frac{5}{6} - \frac{2}{6} =$

10. $\frac{2}{7} + \frac{4}{7} =$

11. $\frac{10}{11} - \frac{7}{11} =$

12. $\frac{2}{14} - \frac{1}{14} =$

13. $\frac{1}{3} + \frac{1}{3} =$

14. $\frac{5}{25} + \frac{10}{25} =$

SOLVE on Your Own

Skills Practice

Add or subtract the fractions.
Simplify if possible.

Remember when adding or subtracting like fractions, to add or subtract the numerators while keeping the denominator the same.

1. $\frac{10}{12} + \frac{2}{12}$ _____

2. $\frac{10}{12} - \frac{2}{12}$ _____

3. $\frac{3}{15} + \frac{5}{15}$ _____

4. $\frac{1}{4} + \frac{2}{4}$ _____

5. $\frac{3}{4} - \frac{1}{4}$ _____

6. $\frac{5}{6} - \frac{3}{6}$ _____

7. $\frac{5}{6} + \frac{1}{6}$ _____

8. $\frac{3}{10} + \frac{2}{10}$ _____

9. $\frac{50}{100} + \frac{50}{100}$ _____

10. $\frac{1}{2} - \frac{1}{2}$ _____

11. $\frac{3}{15} + \frac{10}{15}$ _____

12. $\frac{11}{22} - \frac{9}{22}$ _____

13. $\frac{7}{14} + \frac{2}{14}$ _____

14. $\frac{7}{14} - \frac{3}{14}$ _____

15. $\frac{3}{21} + \frac{7}{21}$ _____

Add and Subtract Fractions with Like Denominators

Strategy

Guess, Check, and Revise

Step 1: Read Randy has two blank DVD-RW discs. Each disc holds 8 gigabytes of information. He burned an archive of photographs on the first disc that took up $2\frac{3}{4}$ gigabytes. On a second disc, he burned an archive that took up $3\frac{1}{4}$ gigabytes. Now, he wants to burn one archive that takes up $3\frac{7}{10}$ gigabytes, two archives that take up $1\frac{3}{5}$ gigabytes each, and a smaller archive that takes up $\frac{3}{4}$ gigabytes. On which discs should he burn which archives so that all of them fit?

STRATEGY	SOLUTION
Guess, Check, and Revise Guessing is a good way to start problems dealing with measurement. You can then do the math to check your guess. Then revise it if needed.	Step 2: Plan Estimate the space left on each disc and the size of each archive to burn. Arrange the archives so that their total space is less than the remaining space on the disc. Step 3: Solve Disc 1 has about 3 gigabytes already used, so it has about 5 gigabytes left. Disc 2 has about $3\frac{1}{2}$ gigabytes burned so it has about $4\frac{1}{2}$ gigabytes left. The new archives are about 4, 2, 2, and 1 gigabytes in size, so he can put the first and last archives **or** the 2nd and 3rd archives on Disc 1 (and the other photographs on Disc 2). Step 4: Check Disc 1 contains archives of sizes $2\frac{3}{4} + 3\frac{7}{10} + \frac{3}{4} = 3\frac{1}{2} + 3\frac{7}{10} = 7\frac{2}{10} = 7\frac{1}{5}$. Disc 2 has archives of sizes $3\frac{1}{4} + 1\frac{3}{5} + 1\frac{3}{5} = 3\frac{1}{4} + 2\frac{6}{5} = 3\frac{1}{4} + 3\frac{1}{5} = 6\frac{9}{20}$.

Choose the Right Word

composite number   improper fraction   factor

Fill in each blank with the correct word or phrase from the box.

1. A(n) _____ has a numerator that is greater than the denominator.

2. A number that divides evenly into another number is a(n) _____ of that number.

3. A number that has more than itself and one as factors is a(n) _____.

Yes or No?

Answer these questions and be ready to explain your answers.

4. Since two is an even number, is it also a composite number? _____

5. Can composite numbers have less than three factors? _____

6. Is a factor of a number that is not the number itself smaller than that number? _____

7. Is a multiple of a number that is not the number itself greater than that number? _____

Show That You Know

Compute the sums.

8. $\frac{1}{4} + \frac{2}{4}$

9. $\frac{1}{2} + \frac{1}{2}$

10. $9\frac{12}{17}$
    $+\ 6\frac{4}{17}$

11. $2\frac{1}{29}$
    $8\frac{18}{29}$
    $+\ \frac{20}{29}$

Compute the differences.

12. $\frac{2}{3} - \frac{1}{3}$

13. $\frac{2}{5} - \frac{1}{5}$

14. $\frac{24}{33}$
    $-\ \frac{18}{33}$

READ on Your Own

Reading Comprehension Strategy: Questioning

Communication and Technology, *pages 6–8*

Before You Read

What did you find most surprising in "Communicating with Koko?"

As You Read

As you read "Instant Messaging," ask yourself questions such as "How does instant messaging work" and "Why do people send instant messages?"

Read "Instant Messaging," pages 6–8. (STOP)

Read the "between-the-lines" question below. Then write the answer.

> **"Between-the-lines" question:**
>
> Is instant messaging always safe?
>
> _____
>
> _____
>
> _____
>
> _____

After You Read

What's the difference between IMing and texting?

_____

_____

SOLVE on Your Own

Communication and Technology, *page 8*

Organize the Information

Use the "Guess, Check, and Revise" strategy to determine how these friends can IM for a total of one hour a day. The limit per IM session is half an hour. Complete the chart with the number of minutes that each pair can IM.

	Tina	Sarah	Yosef	Ralph	Melinda	Total
Tina	---					60
Sarah		---				60
Yosef			---			60
Ralph				---		60
Melinda					---	60
Total	60	60	60	60	60	---

You Do the Math

Use the information in the table above to answer these questions. Write your answers in the space provided.

Remember, there are 60 minutes in an hour.

1. How can you put the minutes from the table in fraction form?

_____

_____

2. How can you simplify your fractions?

_____

3. How can you find how much time was spent IMing for the day?

_____

After You Solve

Would you rather IM or talk on the phone?

_____

_____

The Four-Step Problem-Solving Plan

Step 1: Read	Step 2: Plan	Step 3: Solve	Step 4: Check
Make sure you understand what the problem is asking.	Decide how you will solve the problem.	Solve the problem using your plan.	Check to make sure your answer is correct.

Read the article below. Then answer the questions.

There are roughly 37 million blogs on the Internet, with a new blog created every second. The "blogosphere" or (blog community) doubles in size every six months. It is now 60 times bigger than it was three years ago, with 1.2 million new postings each day. English is not the most popular language of the blogosphere—it's Japanese. Thirty-seven percent of blogs are written in Japanese, 31 percent in English, and 15 percent in Chinese. The remaining percentage of blogs are written in other languages.

According to one study, blogs have a large effect on society. The study found that while bloggers make up a small portion of overall Internet users, they are starting to take over public discussions, or talks. Bloggers have also affected what people buy. For instance, music companies are allowing bloggers to use their music for free when bloggers discuss their favorite music groups. When a blogger adds music to a blog, other readers hear it. This helps the music companies sell more music.

1. How has the use of blogging changed?

_____

_____

_____

2. What percent of bloggers write in a language other than Japanese, English, or Chinese?

_____

_____

_____

YOUR TURN

Read the article below. Then answer the questions.

Blog Subject Matter

When bloggers were asked to pick the one topic on which they blogged the most often, 37 percent named their own life experiences. Politics and government came in second place, with 11 percent of bloggers saying that public life was their main subject. Seven percent named entertainment-related topics as their main topic lines, followed by 6 percent naming sports, 5 percent naming current events, and 4 percent naming technology. Two percent of blogs discussed spirituality. Other topics included hobbies, health problems, opinions, and education.

Bloggers can discuss any concerns they have on any topic in a public forum that allows others to comment. They can use their blogs as a way to develop awareness, connect with others who share similar ideas, and call attention to injustices they feel might otherwise be overlooked.

1. What percent shows the difference between the number of bloggers who write about their life experiences and the number of bloggers who write about politics?

   _____

2. What percent of bloggers write about sports and technology?

   _____

3. Why does blogging attract so many people with diverse interests?

   _____

   _____

   _____

Fluency Tip

Remember that colons, semicolons, and commas are guides that tell you when to pause as you are reading.

READ on Your Own

Reading Comprehension Strategy: Questioning

Communication and Technology, *pages 9–11*

VOCABULARY

Watch for the words you are learning about.

precautions: things done to prevent something dangerous or unpleasant from happening

Fluency Tip

Read the text more than once. You will read more smoothly and you will be more likely to remember what you read.

Before You Read

Consider what you read about in "Instant Messaging." How does instant messaging differ from the bulletin boards and chat rooms of an earlier generation?

As You Read

Preview pages 9–11 of "Blogging—A Favorite Pastime."

In the first column of the chart, jot down three to five questions that come to mind as you read the article.

Carefully read pages 9–11 of "Blogging—A Favorite Pastime." STOP

In the second column of the chart, jot down answers you found in the reading. Some questions may not have an answer in the reading.

What Will I Learn?	Answers I Found in the Reading
_____	_____
_____	_____
_____	_____
_____	_____
_____	_____
_____	_____

After You Read

What type of blog would you create? Explain your answer.

_____

_____

_____

SOLVE on Your Own

Communication and Technology, *page 12*

Organize the Information

Use a table like the one below to organize the information you find in the Math Project on magazine page 12.

Frequency of Blogging	Number of Friends	Fraction of Friends
Every day	1	$\frac{1}{12}$
Only on weekends	8	
Three days a week	2	
Only on weekdays	1	

Math Project

Use the information in the table above to answer these questions. Write your answers in the space provided.

In this problem, if you get an answer greater than 1, you know you have made a mistake.

1. How will you add fractions?

_____

2. How will you subtract fractions?

_____

3. How will you simplify your fractions?

_____

After You Solve

What other strategy could you use to solve this problem? Explain.

_____

_____

_____

Adding and Subtracting Fractions with Unlike Denominators

Learn the SKILL

Karen and Jane are comparing the e-mails they got on Tuesday. Karen had 12 new e-mails in her inbox. Of these, four were junk mail. Jane had six e-mails, and three of them were junk mail. What is the total fraction of junk e-mails the girls got? Which girl had a greater fraction of junk e-mails, and by how much?

Fluency Tip

Try reading the text aloud. It will require you to slow down and make sure that you are pronouncing each word correctly. Hearing the words out loud will help you to understand them.

SKILL	EXAMPLE	COMPLETE THE EXAMPLE
In order for fractions to be added or subtracted they have to have the same denominator. If the denominators are different, find a common multiple of both denominators. This can be used as a common denominator. When you change the denominator of a fraction, you must also change the numerator so that the fraction has same value. This is called renaming the fraction.	Rename the fractions $\frac{4}{12}$ and $\frac{3}{6}$ so that they have the same denominator. 12 is a multiple of both 6 and 12, so it is a common denominator. $\frac{4}{12}$, therefore, stays the same. $\frac{3}{6}$ must be renamed. To change the denominator from 6 to 12, you must multiply both the numerator and denominator by 2. $\frac{3}{6} \times \frac{2}{2} = \frac{6}{12}$	Rename the fractions $\frac{1}{4}$ and $\frac{4}{8}$ so that they have the same denominator. _____
Once the denominators are the same, the two fractions can be added or subtracted.	$\frac{4}{12} + \frac{6}{12} = \frac{10}{12}$ $\frac{6}{12} - \frac{4}{12} = \frac{2}{12}$	Add $\frac{2}{8} + \frac{4}{8}$. _____
After adding or subtracting, the resulting fraction may need to be simplified.	$\frac{10}{12} = \frac{5}{6}$ $\frac{2}{12} = \frac{1}{6}$	Simplify $\frac{6}{8}$. _____

Choose the Right Word

multiple   rename   numerator
denominator

Fill in each blank with the correct word or phrase from the box.

1. The _____ is the top part of the fraction.

2. To _____ is to show a number in another way.

3 The _____ is the bottom part of the fraction.

4. A _____ is a product of one number and another whole number.

Yes or No?

Answer these questions and be ready to explain your answers.

5. If you add two fractions with different denominators, do you add the denominators? _____

6. If you have to change the denominator to rename a fraction, does the numerator also have to be changed? _____

7. Is it possible to add $\frac{1}{2}$ and $\frac{3}{4}$? _____

8. Is it always possible to simplify a fraction? _____

Show That You Know

Rename the fractions to have common denominators.

9. $\frac{5}{6}$ and $\frac{2}{3}$

10. $\frac{5}{6}$ and $\frac{2}{12}$

11. $\frac{2}{4}$ and $\frac{1}{3}$

Add or subtract the fractions. Simplify if possible.

12. $\frac{10}{5} - \frac{7}{10} =$

13. $\frac{2}{7} - \frac{1}{14} =$

14. $\frac{1}{9} + \frac{1}{3} =$

15. $\frac{5}{5} + \frac{10}{25} =$

SOLVE on Your Own

Skills Practice
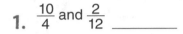

Rename the fractions so they have the same denominators.

When one denominator is a factor of the other, the larger denominator is a common denominator.

1. $\frac{10}{4}$ and $\frac{2}{12}$ _____

2. $\frac{10}{2}$ and $\frac{2}{6}$ _____

3. $\frac{3}{15}$ and $\frac{3}{5}$ _____

4. $\frac{1}{3}$ and $\frac{2}{4}$ _____

5. $\frac{3}{24}$ and $\frac{1}{16}$ _____

9. $\frac{50}{50} + \frac{50}{100} =$ _____

10. $\frac{1}{2} - \frac{1}{4} =$ _____

11. $\frac{3}{15} + \frac{10}{3} =$ _____

Add or subtract the fractions. Simplify if possible.

12. $\frac{11}{2} - \frac{4}{1} =$ _____

6. $\frac{5}{3} - \frac{3}{6} =$ _____

13. $\frac{7}{14} + \frac{2}{7} =$ _____

7. $\frac{5}{6} + \frac{3}{2} =$ _____

14. $\frac{7}{2} - \frac{3}{14} =$ _____

8. $\frac{3}{10} + \frac{2}{20} =$ _____

15. $\frac{3}{7} + \frac{7}{3} =$ _____

Adding and Subtracting Fractions with Unlike Denominators

Strategy

Try a Simpler Form of the Problem

Step 1: Read Karen's skirt measures $30\frac{1}{3}$ inches long. She wants to take $4\frac{1}{4}$ inches off the length and add a decorative hem that is $2\frac{4}{5}$ inches wide. How long will the altered skirt be?

STRATEGY	SOLUTION

Try a Simpler Form of the Problem

Using estimation to make a problem simpler is a good way to start problems that involve measurement. First, round any mixed numbers to the nearest whole numbers, then calculate the final estimated measurement.

Then do the math and check the answer against your estimate to see if your answer is reasonable.

Step 2: Plan First, round each number to estimate how long the skirt will be after Karen shortens it and then adds the new hem.

30 inches − 4 inches + 3 inches is 29 inches.

The new length of the skirt should be about 29 inches.

Step 3: Solve Subtract $4\frac{1}{4}$ inches from the initial length, $30\frac{1}{3}$ inches.

$$30\frac{1}{3} - 4\frac{1}{4}$$

To subtract fractions, rename to common denominators.

$$30\frac{4}{12} - 4\frac{3}{12} = 26\frac{1}{12}$$

Now add the hem, $2\frac{4}{5}$ inches, to $26\frac{1}{12}$.

$$26\frac{1}{12} + 2\frac{4}{5}$$

To add fractions, rename to common denominators. Find a common multiple of 12 and 5. The least common multiple is 60, so rename the fractions to make 60 the denominator.

$$26\frac{5}{60} + 2\frac{48}{60} = 28\frac{53}{60}$$

Step 4: Check The skirt will be $28\frac{53}{60}$ inches long. This rounds to 29 inches, which matches the estimate. Therefore, $28\frac{53}{60}$ inches is a reasonable answer.

YOUR TURN

Choose the Right Word

> factor numerator multiple

Fill in each blank with the correct word or phrase from the box.

1. The _____ is the number above the denominator.

2. A number that a smaller number divides evenly into is a _____ of that number.

3. A number that divides evenly into a larger number is a _____ of that number.

Yes or No?

Answer these questions and be ready to explain your answers.

4. When subtracting fractions, should you first change the denominators to be the same? _____

5. When adding mixed numbers, should you first change the denominators to be the same? _____

6. Can simplifying one or more of the fractions help you find common denominators? _____

Show That You Know

Add the fractions. Simplify if possible.

7. $\frac{7}{8} + \frac{3}{4}$

8. $\frac{4}{5} + \frac{1}{2}$

9. $\frac{7}{8} + \frac{2}{16}$

10. $\frac{12}{24} + \frac{18}{36}$

Subtract the fractions. Simplify if possible.

11. $\frac{3}{4} - \frac{1}{2}$

12. $\frac{6}{8} - \frac{2}{4}$

13. $\frac{2}{3} - \frac{1}{2}$

14. Find a common denominator of $\frac{1}{4}$ and $\frac{2}{3}$.

15. Find a common denominator of $\frac{5}{6}$ and $\frac{1}{9}$.

READ on Your Own

Reading Comprehension Strategy: Questioning

Communication and Technology, *pages 13–15*

Before You Read

You read about blogs in "Blogging—a Favorite Pastime." Why might you want to see someone's photoblog?

As You Read

Preview the diagram and bold vocabulary words in "Are Computers Safe?" on pages 13–15.

Write a goal-setting question in the chart below.

Now read "Are Computers Safe?" on pages 13–15.

Write a details question in the chart. Then write answers to your questions.

Before You Read	After You Read
Goal-setting question: _____ _____ _____	_____ _____ _____
Details question: _____ _____ _____	_____ _____ _____

After You Read

How do businesses and homes protect their computers?

_____

_____

VOCABULARY

Watch for the words you are learning about.

access: a way to enter into a place

authorization: permission to do something

computer virus: a computer program hidden within a seemingly harmless program that causes damage to a computer

firewall: a computer program that limits access by outside users

security: protection for something that is important to you

Fluency Tip

Be careful to read every word without skipping or substituting words. If a sentence or paragraph does not make sense, reread every word.

SOLVE on Your Own

Communication and Technology, *page 15*

Organize the Information

Complete the table.

	First Quarter to Second Quarter	Second Quarter to Third Quarter
Alexis's Stock A	$18\frac{1}{2} - 18\frac{1}{3} = \frac{3}{6} - \frac{2}{6} = $ rise $\frac{1}{6}$	
Ronnell's Stock B		

You Do the Math

Use the information in the table above to answer these questions. Write your answers in the space provided.

Find a common denominator before subtracting.

1. How will you find out how much Alexis's stock and Ronnell's stock went up each quarter?

_____

2. How will you find out which stock rises the most?

_____

_____

_____

After You Solve

What stocks do you know? How do people make money in stocks?

_____

_____

_____

Solve It!

The Four-Step Problem-Solving Plan

Step 1: Read	Step 2: Plan	Step 3: Solve	Step 4: Check
Make sure you understand what the problem is asking.	Decide how you will solve the problem.	Solve the problem using your plan.	Check to make sure your answer is correct.

Read the article below. Then answer the questions.

Cell phones have become such a part of our daily lives that we forget what life was like before they were invented. Before cell phones, there were two options for mobile communication: the walkie-talkie and the CB radio. The origins of cell phone technology can be found in these outdated technologies. To see how far we have come with the cell phone, we must understand how these older communication devices operate.

Technically, cell phones, walkie-talkies, and CB radios are all radios. Walkie-talkies and CB radios allow two people to communicate through one radio frequency. This means that only one person can talk at a time. A cell phone, on the other hand, uses two frequencies: one for talking, and one for listening. This allows two people to talk and listen at the same time.

Another important difference is how the frequencies are sent. CB radios and walkie-talkies use transmitters to send frequencies. Walkie-talkies use a 0.25-watt transmitter, and CB radios use a 5-watt transmitter. Because these transmitters are not very powerful, they cannot send frequencies very far. Cell phones, however, transmit by using cells. As the cell phone moves from one area to another, it switches cells. Since the cells are now spread out over much of the world, they have an incredibly large range.

1. How are cell phones like the CB radios and walkie-talkies of an earlier generation?

_____

_____

_____

_____

2. What is the difference, in watts, between a walkie-talkie transmitter and a CB radio transmitter?

_____

_____

YOUR TURN

Read the article. Then answer the questions.

Digital and PCS Service

There are two types of digital cell services—Digital Cell Service and Personal Communication Services (PCS). Digital cell phones use a mixture of the technology from the older radio system and the digital system. Digital Cell Service uses radio towers to send signals. A call is set up using the normal method and then the conversation itself is sent digitally.

PCS phones use a completely digital system. They use a different set of towers and a different set of higher frequencies. The frequencies range between 1.85 and 2.15 gigahertz (GHz). Because of these higher frequencies, the towers must be built closer together. One result of using a completely digital system is that the sound quality of the calls is much better and clearer. PCS companies are also known for providing services for several of their customers' needs. Instead of being just a phone service, PCS companies usually offer other services like paging, caller ID, and e-mail into their basic packages.

1. How are digital and PCS services alike?

   _____

   _____

2. What is the frequency of a PCS phone that is 0.35 GHz greater than the minimum?

   _____

3. What does the PCS system offer that the traditional digital system does not?

   _____

   _____

Fluency Tip

Take your time when reading complex material so you can make sense of difficult ideas.

READ on Your Own

Reading Comprehension Strategy: Questioning

Communication and Technology, *pages 16–18*

VOCABULARY

Watch for the words you are learning about.

text messages: short notes sent from one cell phone to another

Fluency Tip

Review any words in boldfaced type before you read. Make sure you know how to pronounce these words.

Before You Read

Think about the computer security programs mentioned in "Are Computers Safe?" How might we protect the information we have on our computers?

As You Read

Preview "More Than a Cell Phone," pages 16–18.

Write a goal-setting question and a details question in the chart below.

Read "More Than a Cell Phone," pages 16–18.

Write your answers in the chart below.

Before You Read	After You Read
Goal-setting question: _____ _____ _____	_____ _____ _____
Details question: _____ _____ _____	_____ _____ _____

After You Read

Why do you think many teens rely so heavily on their cell phones?

_____

_____

SOLVE on Your Own

Communication and Technology, *page 19*

Organize the Information

Use a table like the one below to organize the information.

Number of Cell Phone Users in Logan's Class		
Cell Phone Used For	**Fraction**	**Classroom of 24 People**
Making calls only	$\frac{1}{3}$	
Making calls and taking pictures	$\frac{1}{3}$	
Making calls and playing games		
Making calls, taking pictures, and playing games		

Math Project

Use the information in the list above to answer these questions. Write your answers in the space provided.

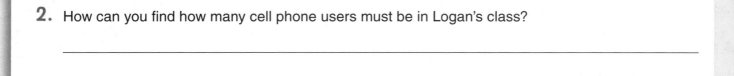

In this problem you could draw a model or use counters to help you.

1. How will you find the fraction of Logan's classmates who use their cell phones for making calls, taking pictures, and playing games?

_____

_____

2. How can you find how many cell phone users must be in Logan's class?

_____

_____

After You Solve

How could you express the same information in the table by drawing a picture? Explain.

_____

_____

Put It Together · · · · · · · · · · · · · · · ·

Introducing Adding and Subtracting Fractional Measures

You have learned how to add and subtract fractions. How can you add and subtract measurements involving fractions?

ADD: $2\frac{1}{2}$ ft $+ 3\frac{3}{4}$ ft

The whole numbers and fractions are added just like in earlier lessons.

Find a common denominator and write equivalent fractions.

$2\frac{2}{4}$ ft $+ 3\frac{3}{4}$ ft $= 5\frac{5}{4}$ ft $= 6\frac{1}{4}$ ft (6 ft 3 in.)

The same problem could also be calculated in feet and inches.

Since 1 ft $= 12$ in., $\frac{1}{2}$ ft $= 6$ in. and $\frac{3}{4}$ ft $= 9$ in.

2 ft 6 in. $+$ 3 ft 9 in. $=$ 5 ft 15 in. $=$ 5 ft $+$ 1 ft $+$ 3 in. $=$ 6 ft 3 in. ($6\frac{1}{4}$ ft)

SUBTRACT: $8\frac{1}{3}$ yd $- 4\frac{5}{6}$ yd

The whole numbers and fractions are subtracted just like whole numbers and fractions in your earlier lessons.

Find a common denominator and write equivalent fractions.

$8\frac{2}{6}$ yd $- 4\frac{5}{6}$ yd $= 7\frac{8}{6} - 4\frac{5}{6}$ yd $= 3\frac{3}{6}$ yd $= 3\frac{1}{2}$ yd

The same problem can also be calculated in smallest units. Since 1 yard $= 36$ in.

$\frac{1}{3}$ yd $= 12$ in. and $\frac{5}{6}$ yd $= 30$ in.

8 yd 12 in. $-$ 4 yd 30 in. $=$ 7 yd 48 in. $-$ 4 yd 30 in. $=$ 3 yd 18 in. ($3\frac{1}{2}$ yd)

Practicing the Algorithm

Add the following measurements.

1. $6\frac{3}{4}$ yd $+ 2\frac{2}{3}$ yd $=$ _____

2. $8\frac{11}{12}$ ft $- 3\frac{5}{12}$ ft $=$ _____

3. $11\frac{1}{6}$ ft $+ 4\frac{3}{4}$ ft $=$ _____

YOUR TURN

Thinking About Adding and Subtracting Fractional Measures

When you add or subtract measures, the measures must be of the same units.

ADD: $3\frac{1}{2}$ quarts + 3 pints

Remember: 1 quart = 2 pints

This problem could be rewritten in quarts: $3\frac{1}{2}$ quarts + $1\frac{1}{2}$ quarts = 5 quarts.

The problem could also be rewritten in pints: 7 pints + 3 pints = 10 pints = 5 quarts.

SUBTRACT: $1\frac{3}{4}$ gallons − 3 quarts

Remember: 1 gallon = 4 quarts

This problem could be rewritten in gallons. $1\frac{3}{4}$ gallons − $\frac{3}{4}$ gallon = 1 gallon.

This problem could be rewritten in quarts. 7 quarts − 3 quarts = 4 quarts = 1 gallon.

Rewriting the problem in smaller units of measure in not always the most convenient way to do computation. When you rewrite a problem using smaller units of measure, the result is always a **greater number of units.**

Jodi lives $3\frac{1}{8}$ miles away from school and Beena lives $1\frac{2}{3}$ miles away from school.

1. How would you find the least possible distance between their homes?

   _____

2. What is the least possible distance?

   _____

3. How would you find the greatest possible distance between their homes?

   _____

4. What is the greatest possible distance?

   _____

5. Why would it not be convenient to rewrite this problem in yards or feet?

   _____

> **Tip** When you add and subtract fractions, think about how many parts there are in the whole.

Show That You Know

Read the information below. Use what you read about addition and multiplication to answer the questions. Remember what you have learned in this lesson about multiplication. Use the space provided to show your work.

Mary Beth kept a record of the time she spent on the computer for five days last week. She worked on homework assignments that required research on the Internet. She also e-mailed friends, downloaded music, and ordered a book for her sister's birthday present, played a computer game, and wrote a research paper.

The chart shows the time (in hours) spent on each activity.

Time Spent on Computer (in hours)

	Mon.	Tues.	Wed.	Thurs.	Fri.
Research	$1\frac{1}{2}$	$\frac{2}{3}$	$\frac{1}{2}$	$2\frac{1}{4}$	$\frac{3}{4}$
E-mail	$\frac{1}{4}$	$\frac{1}{4}$	$\frac{1}{5}$	$\frac{1}{4}$	$1\frac{1}{3}$
Download music	$\frac{3}{4}$		$\frac{3}{4}$	2	
Order present					$\frac{1}{4}$
Computer games		$\frac{3}{4}$			
Writing	$1\frac{3}{4}$	$\frac{3}{4}$	$1\frac{1}{4}$		$1\frac{5}{6}$

1. On which day did she spend the least amount of time using the computer? How many hours did she spend on the computer that day? How many minutes?

2. How many hours did she spend downloading music during the week?

Show That You Know (continued)

3. On which item did she spend the most time during the week? How many hours did she spend on the item? How many minutes?

4. How many more hours during the week did she spend using email than playing computer games?

5. How many more hours did Mary Beth spend on the computer on Thursday than on Tuesday?

6. What is the total time Mary Beth spent on the computer during the week?

7. Express Mary Beth's time on the computer in hours and minutes.

Review What You've Learned

8. What have you learned in this Connections lesson about adding and subtracting fractional measures?

_____

9. What have you learned in this Connections lesson that you did not already know?

_____

10. What have you learned in this lesson that will help you further understand operations using fractions?

_____

_____

Review and Practice

Skills Review

Prime numbers and composite numbers:

The only **factors** of a **prime number** are 1 and the number itself. 19 is an example.

Composite numbers have 3 or more factors.

Eight is a **composite number**; its factors are 1, 2, 4, 8.

Common factors and multiples:

The **factors** for 10 are 1, 2, 5, 10.

The **factors** for 25 are: 1, 5, 25.

The greatest common factor is 5.

Multiplying a number and whole number gives a **multiple** of the number.

The least common multiple of 15 and 25 is 75, because $15 \times 5 = 75$ and $25 \times 3 = 75$.

Adding fractions with like denominators:

When two fractions have the same **denominator**, addition problems are calculated by adding the **numerators**.

$\frac{2}{14} + \frac{5}{14} = \frac{7}{14}$

$\frac{7}{14}$ simplifies to $\frac{1}{2}$

Subtracting fractions with like denominators:

When two fractions have the same **denominator**, subtraction problems are calculated by subtracting the **numerators**.

$\frac{2}{9} - \frac{1}{9} = \frac{1}{9}$

Adding fractions with unlike denominators:

Rename the fractions using least common multiples, so the **denominators** are alike.

$\frac{3}{4} + \frac{1}{8} = \frac{6}{8} + \frac{1}{8} = \frac{7}{8}$

Subtracting fractions with unlike denominators:

Rename the fractions using least common multiples, so the **denominators** are alike.

$\frac{5}{6} - \frac{8}{12} = \frac{10}{12} - \frac{8}{12} = \frac{2}{12} = \frac{1}{6}$

Strategy Review

- When finding common factors (or multiples) of two numbers, first list all the factors (or multiples) for each number. Then compare the numbers in each list.

- Make initial estimates of solutions to addition problems with fractions. The actual answer should be close to the estimate.

- Also make initial estimates of solutions to subtraction problems involving fractions.

Skills and Strategies Practice

Complete the exercises below.

1. Which of the following is a prime number?

   15, 10, 27, 29, 30

   _____

4. $\frac{7}{17} + \frac{6}{17} =$ _____

2. What are two common factors of 24 and 60?

   _____

5. $\frac{7}{17} - \frac{6}{17} =$ _____

3. Make an estimate of the sum of $\frac{4}{9}$ and $\frac{2}{10}$.

   _____

6. $\frac{1}{3} - \frac{1}{4} =$ _____

TEST-TAKING tip

When you study for a math test, review any formulas and example problems. Then practice the step-by-step procedures for solving problems. For a problem like $\frac{2}{3} + \frac{5}{27}$, go through a series of steps. First, see if the denominators are the same. Since they are not, ask yourself what to do to make the denominators the same. In this case, you should find the least common multiple, 27. Then, change the first fraction so that the denominators of both fractions are the same: $\frac{2}{3} = \frac{18}{27}$. Next, add the numerators, then simplify the solution, if possible: $\frac{18}{27} + \frac{5}{27} = \frac{23}{27}$.

Mid-Unit Review

Circle the letter of the correct answer.

1. Which of the following is a prime number?

    A. 4   C. 6

    B. 5   D. 9

2. What are all the factors of 16?

    A. 1, 16

    B. 1, 2, 4, 8, 16

    C. 1, 2, 4, 16

    D. 1, 2, 3, 4, 12, 16

3. $\frac{11}{12} - \frac{8}{12} =$ _____

    A. $\frac{1}{3}$ C. $\frac{1}{4}$

    B. $\frac{1}{5}$ D. $\frac{1}{8}$

4. $\frac{1}{10} + \frac{4}{5} =$ _____

    A. $\frac{5}{10}$ C. $\frac{8}{10}$

    B. $\frac{18}{10}$ D. $\frac{9}{10}$

5. $\frac{1}{2} - \frac{4}{12} =$ _____

    A. $\frac{1}{6}$ C. $\frac{3}{12}$

    B. $\frac{1}{3}$ D. $\frac{1}{12}$

6. $\frac{2}{6} + \frac{3}{30} =$ _____

    A. $\frac{15}{30}$ C. $\frac{1}{3}$

    B. $\frac{13}{30}$ D. $\frac{1}{6}$

7. What is the greatest common factor of 12 and 36?

    A. 36   C. 3

    B. 4   D. 12

8. $\frac{8}{9} - \frac{7}{18} =$ _____

    A. $\frac{8}{18}$ C. $\frac{1}{2}$

    B. $\frac{4}{9}$ D. $\frac{15}{18}$

9. What number is a multiple of 11?

    A. 131   C. 21

    B. 111   D. 33

10. $\frac{2}{3}$ is the same as:

    A. $\frac{3}{2}$ C. $\frac{6}{6}$

    B. $\frac{6}{9}$ D. $\frac{9}{12}$

11. Which of the following is a composite number?

    A. 7   C. 21

    B. 3   D. 17

12. $\frac{9}{17} + \frac{7}{17} =$ _____

    A. $\frac{2}{17}$ C. 1

    B. $\frac{16}{17}$ D. $\frac{15}{17}$

13. $\frac{5}{15}$ is the same as:

    A. $\frac{10}{25}$ C. $\frac{2}{3}$

    B. $\frac{2}{7}$ D. $\frac{1}{3}$

14. $\frac{6}{43} - \frac{3}{43} =$ _____

    A. $\frac{2}{43}$ C. $\frac{3}{43}$

    B. $\frac{1}{7}$ D. $\frac{9}{43}$

Mid-Unit Review

15. $\frac{10}{25} + \frac{1}{5} =$ _____

A. $\frac{3}{5}$ C. $\frac{4}{5}$

B. $\frac{11}{25}$ D. $\frac{20}{25}$

16. What are all the factors of 28?

A. 1, 2, 4, 7, 14, 28

B. 1, 2, 4, 14, 28

C. 2, 4, 7, 14

D. 1, 2, 4, 7, 28

17. $\frac{3}{20} + \frac{4}{20} =$ _____

A. $\frac{1}{20}$ C. $\frac{1}{3}$

B. $\frac{7}{20}$ D. $\frac{1}{5}$

18. $\frac{4}{7} - \frac{1}{3} =$ _____

A. $\frac{6}{21}$ C. $\frac{5}{21}$

B. $\frac{7}{21}$ D. $\frac{8}{14}$

19. What is the least common multiple of 3 and 7?

A. 27   C. 63

B. 42   D. 21

20. $\frac{19}{38}$ is the same as:

A. $\frac{1}{4}$ C. $\frac{1}{3}$

B. $\frac{1}{2}$ D. $\frac{1}{5}$

21. $\frac{4}{5} - \frac{1}{8} =$ _____

A. $\frac{27}{40}$ C. $\frac{7}{10}$

B. $\frac{37}{40}$ D. $\frac{19}{20}$

22. $\frac{1}{22} + \frac{1}{22} =$ _____

A. 0   C. $\frac{1}{11}$

B. $\frac{2}{11}$ D. $\frac{3}{22}$

23. Which is a prime number?

A. 121   C. 13

B. 16   D. 8

24. Which of these numbers is a multiple of 6?

A. 13   C. 19

B. 30   D. 40

25. $\frac{4}{6} - \frac{2}{6} =$ _____

A. $\frac{1}{3}$ C. 1

B. $\frac{2}{3}$ D. $\frac{3}{6}$

26. What is the greatest common factor of 15 and 45?

A. 3   C. 9

B. 5   D. 15

27. $\frac{3}{9} - \frac{1}{3} =$ _____

A. 0   C. $\frac{1}{3}$

B. $\frac{1}{2}$ D. $\frac{2}{3}$

28. Which group has numbers that are all multiples of 30?

A. 30, 40, 50

B. 1, 2, 3, 5, 15, 30

C. 33 and 66

D. 30, 60, 90

29. What is the least common multiple of 4 and 5?

A. 10   C. 40

B. 20   D. 60

Adding Decimals

Learn the SKILL

Jose is 5.3 feet tall. Darren is 4.9 feet tall. What is the total of their heights together?

SKILL	EXAMPLE	COMPLETE THE EXAMPLE
You have already learned how to add multiple digit numbers. To do so, line up the numbers according to place value and add the numbers from right to left.	Find the sum. 53 + 49 Line up the numbers. $\begin{array}{r} 53 \\ + 49 \\ \hline 102 \end{array}$	Find the sum. 104 + 21 _____
When adding decimals, the first step is to line up the decimal points.	Line up the decimal points. $\begin{array}{r} 5.3 \\ + 4.9 \\ \hline \end{array}$	Rewrite the problem so the decimal points line up. 10.4 + 2.1 _____
After the decimals points are lined up, the numbers can be added from right to left. Carry over numbers as needed. Then make sure the decimal point of the sum is lined up with the addends.	Find the sum. 5.3 + 4.9 $\begin{array}{r} 5.3 \\ + 4.9 \\ \hline 10.2 \end{array}$	Find the sum. 10.4 + 2.1 _____

YOUR TURN

Choose the Right Word

addend   decimal   decimal point

Fill in each blank with the correct word or phrase from the box.

1. A(n) _____ is a number that represents part of a whole.

2. A(n) _____ is a number combined with another number to find the total.

3. A(n)_____ separates the digits that represent part of a whole from the digits that represent whole numbers.

Yes or No?

Answer these questions and be ready to explain your answers.

4. Are all the digits lined up according to place value when adding decimals?

    _____

5. Does the decimal point change locations in the solution when adding two decimals?

    _____

6. Is a whole number a decimal? _____

7. Can a decimal be added to itself?

    _____

Show That You Know

Add the decimals.

8. $11.2 + 3.9 =$

9. $5.6 + 2.12 =$

10. $2.4 + 5.3 =$

11. $10.5 + 7.10 =$

12. $2.7 + 1.14 =$

13. $1.9 + 1.3 =$

14. $5.5 + 10.25 =$

SOLVE on Your Own

Skills Practice

Add the decimals.

When the number of digits to the right of the decimal point is not the same in both numbers, you can add zeros to the end of the number with fewer digits so that the place values line up on the right.

1. $10.4 + 2.12 = $ _____

2. $10.2 + 2.6 = $ _____

3. $3.15 + 3.5 = $ _____

4. $1.3 + 2.4 = $ _____

5. $3.24 + 1.4 = $ _____

6. $5.3 + 3.6 = $ _____

7. $5.6 + 3.2 = $ _____

8. $3.10 + 2.20 = $ _____

9. $50.50 + 50.100 = $ _____

10. $1.2 + 1.4 = $ _____

11. $3.15 + 10.3 = $ _____

12. $11.2 + 4.1 = $ _____

13. $7.18 + 2.7 = $ _____

14. $7.2 + 3.14 = $ _____

15. $3.7 + 7.3 = $ _____

Adding Decimals

Strategy

Try a Simpler Form of the Problem

`Step 1: Read` Ben bought 4 used books for the following prices: $1.75, $ 1.25, $1.68, and $4.50. How much did he spend, not including the sales tax?

STRATEGY	SOLUTION
Try a Simpler Form of the Problem Estimating to try a simpler form of the problem is a good way to help solve problems involving money. First round the cents to the nearest dollars. Then use your estimates to help calculate the final amount. You can then do the math and check against your estimate to see if your answer is reasonable.	`Step 2: Plan` Estimate how much the books cost by rounding each price to the nearest dollar. Then add your estimates. `Step 3: Solve` $1.75 = about $2.00 $1.25 = about $1.00 $1.68 = about $2.00 $4.50 = about $5.00 $2.00 + $1.00 + $2.00 + $5.00 = $10.00. Now you know the answer will be close to $10. Next, add the actual amounts. Remember to line up the decimal points. 1.75 1.25 1.68 + 4.50 9.18 `Step 4: Check` $9.18 is the actual amount spent. $9.18 rounds to $9, which is very close to the estimate. Therefore, the answer is reasonable.

> Rounding numbers helps us solve problems using mental math. Rounding is a way to create a simpler form of the problem.

Choose the Right Word

decimal   place value   tenths

Fill in each blank with the correct word or phrase from the box.

1. The _____ separates the whole from the part.

2. The place directly to the right of the decimal point is the _____ place.

3. _____ shows how much a number's position represents.

Yes or No?

Answer these questions and be ready to explain your answers.

4. Should decimals be lined up when adding them? _____

5. Should decimals be lined up when subtracting them? _____

6. Should decimals be lined up by their last digit? _____

7. Can decimals be represented by fractions? _____

Show That You Know

Add the decimals.

8. $1.68 + 1.95 =$

9. $2.34 + 0.66 =$

10. $\$4.32 + \$9.09 + \$2.16 =$

11. $1.99 + 0.51 =$

Add the decimals.

12.
$$\begin{array}{r} 0.01 \\ + \ 0.001 \\ \hline \end{array}$$

13.
$$\begin{array}{r} 2.0002 \\ + \ 0.202 \\ \hline \end{array}$$

14.
$$\begin{array}{r} \$3.14 \\ + \ \$1.01 \\ \hline \end{array}$$

15. $1.2 + 3.4 + 5.6 =$

16. $30.3 + 21.3 + 48.4 =$

READ on Your Own

Reading Comprehension Strategy: Questioning

Communication and Technology, *pages 20–22*

Before You Read

In "More Than a Cell Phone," you read about different ways you can use a cell phone. Try to think of a new way to use cell phones that was not mentioned in the article.

As You Read

Write a goal-setting question in the chart below.

Now read "Text Messaging Takes Over," pages 20–22.

Write a details question in the chart below. Then write answers to your questions.

Before You Read	After You Read
Goal-setting question:	
Details question:	

After You Read

You read about several abbreviations and symbols used in texting. What other texting shortcuts are you familiar with?

SOLVE on Your Own

Communication and Technology, *page 22*

Organize the Information

Complete the chart. You can use the Guess, Check, and Revise strategy to find the different combinations of photos, messages sent, and messages received that total $1.85 in charges.

Item	Cost	First Way		Second Way		Third Way	
		How Many?	Amount	How Many?	Amount	How Many?	Amount
Send message	$0.05						
Receive message	$0.10						
Send or receive photo	$0.25						
Total			$1.85		$1.85		$1.85

You Do the Math

Use the information in the chart above to answer these questions. Write your answers in the space provided.

Once you find one solution, see if you can change it to find a second solution.

1. How will you count the price of the messages?

   _____

2. How will you know how much you have left when you decide on the type of message?

   _____

After You Solve

Can you think of any reasons why a person should not text message?

_____

_____

Subtracting Decimals

Learn the SKILL

Miguel is 5.6 feet tall. Ashley is 5.2 feet tall. Who is taller? By how much is he or she taller?

VOCABULARY

Watch for the words you are learning about.

minuend: number or quantity from which another is subtracted

subtrahend: the number that is subtracted from the minuend

SKILL	EXAMPLE	COMPLETE THE EXAMPLE
You have already learned how to subtract multidigit numbers. To do so, line up the numbers according to place value and subtract the numbers from right to left, regrouping as needed.	Subtract 53 − 49. Line up the numbers. $\begin{array}{r} 53 \\ -\ 49 \\ \hline 4 \end{array}$	Subtract 104 − 21. _____
When subtracting decimals, the first step is to line up the numbers and the decimal points.	Line up the numbers and decimal points. $\begin{array}{r} 5.3 \\ -\ 4.9 \end{array}$	Rewrite the problem so the decimal points are lined up. 10.4 − 2.1 _____
After the decimals points are lined up, the numbers can be subtracted from right to left, regrouping as needed. The decimal point is then lined up with the **minuend** and **subtrahend** in the difference.	Subtract 5.3 − 4.9. $\begin{array}{r} 5.3 \\ -\ 4.9 \\ \hline 0.4 \end{array}$	Subtract 10.4 − 2.1. _____

YOUR TURN

Choose the Right Word

> minuend   subtrahend   decimal
> decimal point

Fill in each blank with the correct word or phrase from the box.

1. A_____ is the point in a decimal.

2. The _____ is the number from which another number is subtracted.

3. The _____ is the number that is subtracted.

4. A_____ is part of a whole.

Yes or No?

Answer these questions and be ready to explain your answers.

5. Is the subtrahend subtracted from the minuend? _____

6. Does the decimal point change locations in the solution when subtracting two decimals? _____

7. Does subtraction go from left to right when subtracting decimals? _____

8. Can a decimal be subtracted from a whole number? _____

Show That You Know

Subtract the decimals.

9. 11.2 − 3.9 =

10. 5.6 − 2.12 =

11. 12.4 − 5.3 =

12. 10.5 − 7.10 =

13. 2.7 − 1.14 =

14. 1.9 − 1.3 =

15. 15.5 − 10.25 =

Unit 3, Lesson 13   149

SOLVE on Your Own

Skills Practice

It can be very helpful with decimals to check your subtraction by adding.

Subtract the decimals.

1. 10.4 − 2.12 = _____

2. 10.2 − 2.6 = _____

3. 3.7 − 3.5 = _____

4. 11.3 − 2.4 = _____

5. 3.24 − 1.4 = _____

6. 5.3 − 3.6 = _____

7. 5.6 − 3.2 = _____

8. 3.10 − 2.20 = _____

9. 150.50 − 50.100 = _____

10. 1.84 − 1.4 = _____

11. 13.15 − 10.3 = _____

12. 11.2 − 4.1 = _____

13. 7.14 − 2.7 = _____

14. 7.2 − 3.14 = _____

15. 10.7 − 7.3 = _____

Subtracting Decimals
Strategy
Guess, Check, and Revise

Step 1: Read Jen had $507.35 in her bank account. She used $135.80 from the account to buy books for school. How much is left in the account?

STRATEGY	SOLUTION
Guess, Check, and Revise Estimating is a good way to help make a guess about the answer. Round the money amounts to various places (nearest hundred dollars, nearest ten dollars, and so on). Then use your estimates to make a guess about the final amount. You can do the math to check your guess. Then revise it if needed.	Step 2: Plan Use estimation to get as close as you can to the difference. This will help you make an educated guess. Step 3: Solve Make an initial guess by rounding each amount of money to the nearest hundred. $507.35 rounds to $500. $135.80 rounds to $100. You can make an initial guess that Jen should have about $400 remaining. Furthermore, since you underestimated both amounts, you can guess that the difference is slightly less than $400. To get a more accurate guess, you can round the nearest ten dollars. $507.35 rounds to $510. $135.80 rounds to $140. Re-estimating the amounts gives you a second guess: Jen should have about $370 remaining. This is quite close. Subtract the original amounts. Remember to line up the decimals. $507.35 − $135.80 $371.55 Step 4: Check Jen has $371.55 remaining, which rounds to $370. Therefore, the guess is reasonable.

YOUR TURN

Choose the Right Word

> tenths   hundredths   ones

Fill in each blank with the correct word or phrase from the box.

1. The _____ place is just to the right of the decimal point.

2. The _____ place is just to the left of the decimal point.

3. The _____ place is two places to the right of the decimal point.

Yes or No?

Answer these questions and be ready to explain your answers.

4. Should decimal points be lined up when subtracting decimals? _____

5. Is the tens place to the right of the decimal point? _____

6. Can decimals be converted to fractions? _____

7. Is a decimal another form of a fraction? _____

Show That You Know

Subtract the decimals.

8. $1.67 - 1.05$

9. $1.34 - 0.75$

10. $\$5.01 - \$2.60$

11. $1.99 - 0.51$

Subtract the decimals.

12. $6.50 - 1.50$

13. $2.0002 - 0.202$

14. $\$4.53$
    $- \ 1.01$

15. 50.65
    $- \ 35.15$

16. 300.75
    $- \ 250.50$

READ on Your Own

Reading Comprehension Strategy: Questioning

Communication and Technology, *pages 23–24*

VOCABULARY

Watch for the words you are learning about.

engineers: people who are trained to design, build, and use machines, computers, bridges, roads, or other structures

username: part of an e-mail address that identifies the recipient

Fluency Tip

Identify words that you do not know. Find out how to pronounce them before reading.

Before You Read

In "Text Messaging Takes Over," you read about texting. Why do you think texting is so popular?

As You Read

Write a goal-setting question in the chart below.

Now read "E-mail, the Fast Mail," pages 23–24.

Write a details question in the chart below. Then answer your questions.

Before You Read	After You Read
Goal-setting question:	
Details question:	

After You Read

What is a possible disadvantage of using e-mail?

SOLVE on Your Own

Communication and Technology, *page 25*

Organize the Information

Complete the table. You can use the Guess, Check, and Revise Strategy to find ways to add the size of the photos. The total should be less than, but close to, 5MB. Can you find a way to send all of the photos in only two e-mails?

	First	Second
Size of Attachments	_____ _____ _____ _____	_____ _____ _____ _____
Total		

You Do the Math

Use the information in the table above to answer these questions. Write your answers in the space provided.

Check your addition using subtraction.

1. How much space do you have available to send the photos?

   _____

2. How can you find out how many MB the photos take up in all?

   _____

3. How can you find out if you can send all of the photos in one e-mail?

   _____

   _____

After You Solve

Why might it be important to have parental controls on computers?

_____

_____

Solve It!

The Four-Step Problem-Solving Plan

Step 1: Read	Step 2: Plan	Step 3: Solve	Step 4: Check
Make sure you understand what the problem is asking.	Decide how you will solve the problem.	Solve the problem using your plan.	Check to make sure your answer is correct.

Read the article below. Then answer the questions.

In the past, people with shared hobbies and interests connected by participating in events and clubs, such as craft circles, sport clubs, and game nights. Though people still participate in such activities, special social networking Web sites have made it possible to join clubs and participate in events with other like-minded people from around the world.

One such Web site has built a community of international soccer fans. It helps users connect to other people around the world who share a passion for the game. Currently, half of the members of the online community are from Brazil, but the appeal of an all-soccer social network is that it will cross all nations. Soccer, or football as it is known everywhere else in the world, is the most popular sport in the world, with extremely enthusiastic fans.

Once signed on, members can build their own soccer teams. They can select players from an international list of the world's best soccer players. Players' biographies and performance information are posted along with their photos. Members can assemble various players together to form their own "dream team." It is a type of fantasy soccer that is now being played across the world.

1. What would be a benefit of joining an online soccer community?

   _____

   _____

   _____

   _____

   _____

2. If $\frac{1}{8}$ of the online soccer community is from the U.S., what fraction names the community from Brazil and the U.S.?

   _____

YOUR TURN

Read the article below. Then answer the questions.

All Soccer, All the Time

Some of the other benefits of being a member of an international online soccer community include access to special content such as soccer profiles, international video clips, and photographs. Members can also add their own pictures, videos, and blogs. Through these features, members can make friends with other soccer fans living across the globe.

In addition to making new friends from other countries, members may use the community to find local soccer teams to join. Soccer lovers and members have arranged real-life teams and met at local parks for tournaments. This brings the social network together. Members have evolved from strangers seated in front of their computer screens, to people getting to know each other in person, bonding over a shared love of the world's most popular sport.

Fluency Tip

As you read and reread, choose a pace that lets you understand what you read.

1. How does the Web site appeal to soccer lovers?

_____

_____

_____

_____

2. One-half of a dream soccer team's players come from Brazil, $\frac{1}{3}$ come from Italy, and the rest come from Germany. Which fraction shows how many of the soccer players come from Germany?

_____

_____

_____

3. How has social networking evolved beyond the original intent?

_____

_____

_____

_____

READ on Your Own

Reading Comprehension Strategy: Questioning

Communication and Technology, *pages 26–28*

VOCABULARY

Watch for the words you are learning about.

acquainted: to know someone, but not very well

Fluency Tip

Change your volume and expression to emphasize parts of the text that are dramatic.

Before You Read

Think about the creation of e-mail in "E-mail, the Fast Mail." Do you think e-mail is more convenient than traditional letter writing?

As You Read

Think about "question words," questions that ask *Who? What? When? Where? Why?* and *How?,* as you read. Place sticky notes next to the answers.

Read "Social Networking," pages 26–28. STOP

Write down a "question word" question in the chart below. Then write the answer when you find it.

Online Social Networking
"Question word" question:
_____
_____
Answer:
_____
_____

After You Read

Why do people enjoy social networking?

_____

_____

_____

SOLVE on Your Own

Communication and Technology, *page 29*

Organize the Information

Use the Draw a Picture strategy to organize the information you find in the Math Project on magazine page 29.

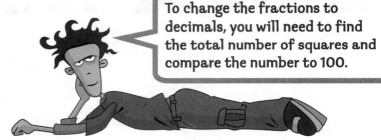

To change the fractions to decimals, you will need to find the total number of squares and compare the number to 100.

Math Project

Use the information in the picture above to answer these questions. Write your answers in the space provided.

1. How did you make a 15 × 20 grid?

_____

2. How will you find decimals for each part of the page?

_____

After You Solve

How could you express the same information in the picture by writing a number sentence?

_____

_____

_____

_____

Estimating Fractional and Decimal Sums and Differences

Learn the SKILL

Mrs. Aronson found that one of the fossils in her collection weighs 0.681 kilogram. A second fossil weighs 0.532 kilogram. What is the total weight of both fossils? What is the difference? Estimate the decimals to find the answers.

SKILL	EXAMPLE	COMPLETE THE EXAMPLE
The numbers to the right of a decimal point can be simplified by rounding to the nearest whole number, tenth, hundredth, and so on. Then the two decimals can be added or subtracted.	Estimate each value to the nearest tenth. $0.532 + 0.681$ 0.532 rounds to 0.5 0.681 rounds to 0.7 $0.5 + 0.7 = 1.2$	Estimate each value to the nearest tenth and then subtract. $0.697 - 0.125$ _____
Fractions can be estimated by using a number line. First, identify two numbers on the number line that the fraction lands between that can be easily converted into decimals. Then, calculate the decimal that is halfway between these and substitute it for the fraction.	Estimate the decimal value for the sum. $\frac{3}{8} + 0.2$ We know $\frac{3}{8}$ is between $\frac{2}{8} = 0.25$, and $\frac{4}{8} = 0.5$. 0.375 is halfway between 0.25 and 0.5. $0.375 + 0.2 = 0.575$. Therefore, $\frac{3}{8} + 0.2$ is about 0.575.	Estimate the decimal value for the difference. $\frac{7}{8} - 0.6$ _____
Fractions can also be estimated by rounding the numerator or denominator to a compatible number. Then, the fractions can be converted to a decimal and added or subtracted.	Estimate the decimal value for the sum. $\frac{12}{52} + 0.532$ The nearest compatible number to $\frac{12}{52}$ is $\frac{13}{52}$. $\frac{13}{52} = \frac{1}{4} = 0.25$ 0.532 can be rounded to 0.53. $0.25 + 0.53 = 0.78$ So, $\frac{12}{52} + 0.532$ is about 0.78.	Estimate the decimal value for the sum. $\frac{8}{28} + 0.5$ _____

YOUR TURN

Choose the Right Word

> estimate   rounding   number line
> compatible number

Fill in each blank with the correct word or phrase from the box.

1. To _____ is to give an answer that is close to the correct answer.

2. A(n) _____ has numbers that are shown as points on a line.

3. A(n) _____ is a number that is easy to compute mentally.

4. Changing a number to the nearest ten, hundred, or so on is called _____.

Yes or No?

Answer these questions and be ready to explain your answers.

5. Is 1.375 rounded to the nearest tenth 1.38? _____

6. Is $\frac{7}{35}$ a good compatible number for $\frac{7}{45}$? _____

7. Can you use a number line to estimate the decimal value of a fraction? _____

8. Can you find a compatible number for $\frac{8}{31}$? _____

Show That You Know

Estimate. Round all decimals to the nearest tenth.

9. $0.475 - 0.279 =$

10. $1.8936 + 2.3456 =$

11. $0.222 + 1.579 =$

12. $\frac{5}{8} + 0.2$

13. $\frac{17}{32} - 0.384$

SOLVE on Your Own

Skills Practice

Remember, when rounding to the nearest tenth, look at the digit in the hundredths place.

Estimate all decimal amounts. Round to the nearest tenth.

1. $0.33 + 0.5432 =$ _____

2. $1.7665 - 0.7659 =$ _____

3. $0.7592 + 0.592 =$ _____

4. $0.21 - 0.135 =$ _____

5. $1.929292 - 1.121212 =$ _____

6. $1.11111111 + 1.1111111 =$ _____

7. $2.1111111 - 1.111111 =$ _____

8. $0.191 + 0.389 =$ _____

9. $6.8059 - 3.7834 =$ _____

10. $9.9219879 + 1.0 =$ _____

11. $5.135 + 2.39 =$ _____

12. $9.511 - 7.3211156 =$ _____

13. $\frac{9}{10} + 0.2 =$ _____

14. $\frac{8}{15} - 0.2 =$ _____

15. $\frac{14}{16} + 0.2 =$ _____

16. $\frac{11}{43} + 0.5 =$ _____

17. $\frac{4}{10} - 0.25 =$ _____

18. $\frac{103}{100} - 1.0 =$ _____

19. $\frac{13}{25} + 0.8 =$ _____

20. $\frac{6}{16} - 0.1 =$ _____

Estimating Fractional and Decimal Sums and Differences

Strategy

Try a Simpler Form of the Problem

Step 1: Read Tina bought 4 buttons at 75 cents each. If she started with $11.95, about how much did she have left?

STRATEGY	SOLUTION
Try a Simpler Form of the Problem Estimating with money is a good way to try a simpler form of the problem to get an idea about the answer. First round fractions of a dollar to the nearest dollar, and add them to get an estimated answer. You can do the math and check against your estimate to see if your answer is reasonable.	**Step 2: Plan** Make an initial estimate by rounding each price to the nearest dollar. Then add. **Step 3: Solve** $\frac{75}{100} = \frac{3}{4}$ $\frac{3}{4}$ rounds to 1. There were 4 buttons, so $1 + 1 + 1 + 1 = 4$. $11.95 rounds to $12.00. $12.00 − $4.00 is $8.00. Therefore, Tina has about $8.00 remaining. Now calculate how much Tina really has. $\frac{3}{4} + \frac{3}{4} + \frac{3}{4} + \frac{3}{4} = \frac{12}{4}$ $\frac{12}{4} = 3$ The buttons cost $3.00 Subtract $3.00 from the initial amount, $11.95. $\quad$ $11.95 $\underline{-\ \$3.00}$ $\quad$ $8.95 **Step 4: Check** Tina has $8.95 remaining. The actual amount is close to the estimate, so your answer is reasonable.

YOUR TURN

Choose the Right Word

estimate   sum   difference

Fill in each blank with the correct word or phrase from the box.

1. The _____ is the result of an addition problem.

2. The _____ is the result of a subtraction problem.

3. To guess the sum or difference of a problem is to _____.

Yes or No?

Answer these questions and be ready to explain your answers.

4. Does $1\frac{1}{2}$ round to 1? _____

5. Does the term difference refer to the answer to an addition problem? _____

6. Does the term round mean to look for the closest whole number? _____

7. Can a decimal be converted into a fraction? _____

8. Does estimating mean you don't have to work out the actual answer? _____

Show That You Know

Estimate. Then round the sums to the nearest whole number.

9. $1.67 + 1.05$

10. $1.34 + 0.75$

11. $\frac{4}{5} + 1\frac{1}{3}$

12. $\frac{9}{10} + 5\frac{1}{2}$

Estimate. Then round the differences to the nearest whole number.

13. $9.25 - 3.25$

14. $4\frac{1}{2} - 1\frac{1}{3}$

15. $4.53 - 1.01$

16. $5\frac{1}{5} - 3\frac{4}{5}$

17. $300.75 - 210.50$

READ on Your Own

Reading Comprehension Strategy: Questioning

Communication and Technology, *pages 30–31*

Before You Read

In "Social Networking," you read about personal Web pages. Have you visited a friend's Web page? What did you like about it? What would you change?

As You Read

As you read "Podcasting" and "Vodcasting," ask yourself questions like *What are they?, How are they the same?, and How are they different?*

Read "Webcasting," pages 30–31.

Write a the "between-the-lines" question below. Then write the answer.

> **"Between-the-lines" question:**
>
> _____
>
> _____
>
> **Answer:**
>
> _____
>
> _____

After You Read

How is podcasting used in schools?

_____

_____

_____

VOCABULARY

Watch for the words you are learning about.

hardware: any computer equipment that can be touched, such as a hard drive, printer, monitor, or keyboard

podcast: an audio program that you can listen to by downloading to a computer or MP3 player

vodcast: an video program that you can listen to by downloading to a computer or MP3 player

webcast: a streaming video or audio program that you can watch or listen to while logged on to the Internet

Fluency Tip

Skim the passage for words that are hard to pronounce. Practice reading those words ahead of time.

SOLVE on Your Own

Communication and Technology, *page 32*

Organize the Information

Complete the table. In the "Positive Reviews" column, find $\frac{2}{3}$ of the total for the each category. In the "Negative Reviews" column, find $\frac{1}{3}$ of the total for each category.

	Total Number of Reviews	Positive Reviews	Negative Reviews
Comedy	28		
Music	42		
News	35		
Sports	37		
Technology	32		
TV/film	26		
Total	200		

You Do the Math

Use the information in the table above to answer these questions. Write your answers in the space provided.

If the total number of reviews is not divisible by 3, round to the nearest whole number.

1. How will you find the number of positive reviews?

_____

2. How will you find the number of negative reviews?

_____

After You Read

What are the advantages and disadvantages of webcasting?

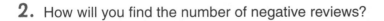

_____

_____

_____

The Four-Step Problem-Solving Plan

Step 1: Read	Step 2: Plan	Step 3: Solve	Step 4: Check
Make sure you understand what the problem is asking.	Decide how you will solve the problem.	Solve the problem using your plan.	Check to make sure your answer is correct.

Read the article below. Then answer the questions.

Have you ever used a computer? Nearly everybody in the United States either owns or has used one by now. Modern computers use Graphical User Interfaces, or GUI, that make interacting with the computer easier via graphical icons or symbols on the screen. But it was not always as easy to get the computer to do what you needed it to!

The first computers filled entire floors of buildings, could only do one thing at a time, and were not at all easy for people to use. They were introduced at the end of World War II to control weapons and radar. Later, they were used to solve complicated problems like forecasting the weather, spacecraft control, and keeping track of inventory. Computers for consumers were first introduced in 1976, but they did not have good graphics and you had to type a series of complex instructions to control them.

Scientists came up with many of the ideas and parts now used in graphical user interfaces in the early 1970s. In 1984, the first personal computer with a GUI was created. Now most computers are based on the same technologies. The big differences are in how they look and how easy they are to use.

1. Which interface is easier to use, typing commands or clicking icons? Why?

   _____

   _____

   _____

2. Why did computers have to get small and have an easy interface before they became popular?

   _____

   _____

   _____

   _____

Read the article below. Then answer the questions.

Where Is the Pointer?

The modern computer interface uses a mouse to move a pointer on a screen. How does moving a mouse make the pointer move?

Usually there is a little ball or light on the bottom of the mouse. When you move the mouse the ball or light moves as well. The mouse has sensors that keep track of the movement. The computer uses the sensor information to calculate how far and in which direction the mouse has been moved from its initial location, or address. The computer's monitor is made up of a collection of pixels, or tiny dots of light, each of which has a corresponding address. As the mouse is moved and its location is changed, the pointer on the monitor moves to match the updated address.

Different monitors may have different numbers of pixels, but graphical programs have to try to look the same on all of them. They do this by converting sizes into portions of screen. An object that takes up half a window will be 200 pixels wide if the window if 400 pixels wide, and it will be 600 pixels wide if the window is 1,200 pixels wide. The only trouble occurs on smaller monitors if the object appears too small to be easy to read or identify.

1. If one window covers 0.36 of the width of the monitor, and another window next to it covers 0.54 of the width of the monitor, what portion of the monitor's width would show the desktop, or background?

_____

_____

_____

_____

2. One monitor is 512 pixels wide and the other is 1024 pixels wide. An object that is exactly 64 pixels wide is displayed on both monitors. On which monitor is the object bigger?

_____

_____

_____

Fluency Tip

To practice reading technical language, pretend you want to sell a computer to a friend and have to read all the specifications.

READ on Your Own

Reading Comprehension Strategy: Questioning

Communication and Technology, *pages 33–35*

VOCABULARY

Watch for the words you are learning about.

interactive: involving an action between people, groups, or things

Fluency Tip

As you read and reread, pay close attention to the words that are difficult to say.

Before You Read

You read about podcasts and vodcasts in "Webcasting." Why would a teacher want to make a podcast or vodcast of a lesson?

As You Read

Read "Interactive Television," on pages 33–35.

For each statement below, explain whether it is true or false and why.

With Interactive TV, you can control the content of a program.

_____

_____

You can participate any time in a synchronized TV show.

_____

_____

A vodcast is an example of participation TV.

_____

_____

After You Read

What is a major drawback of synchronized TV compared to Interactive TV?

_____

_____

_____

SOLVE on Your Own

Communication and Technology, *page 36*

Organize the Information

Read the Math Project on page 36 of the magazine. Complete the chart for Company A. Then complete a similar chart for Company B and Company C.

Programs	Sports	News	Comedies	Dramas	Game Shows	Reality Shows
Decimal	0.10	0.20				
Number of Channels (Total of 150)	15	30				

Math Project

Use the information in the chart above to answer these questions. Write your answers in the space provided.

> Divide the number of channels in each category by the total number to find a decimal for each category.

1. If you start by finding the number of channels, how will you find the decimal for your answer?

_____

_____

2. For every sports channel there are two news channels. If you count the number of news and sports channels, what number will the total be a multiple of? How can this help you answer the question?

_____

_____

_____

After You Solve

Are the total number of channels for the three companies divisible by the same number? How can this help you answer the question?

_____

_____

Put It Together

Introducing Double-Bar and Line Graphs and Coordinate Grids

You have learned about simple bar and line graphs. Bar graphs are used to compare data. A double-bar graph compares amounts from two sets of data. The graphs can be constructed horizontally or vertically. A scale indicating quantity is used on one axis and the bars are identified on the other axis.

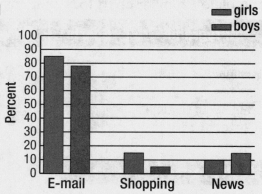

Partial Results of a Survey About Ways Students Use the Internet

Line graphs are used to compare changes over time. The line graph helps you focus on changes and trends. A double-line graph compares the changes over time from two sets of data.

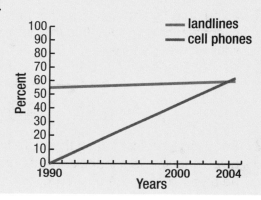

Percent of Households Using Landlines and Cell Phones

Practicing Double-Bar and Line Graphs

What type of graph should you use?

1. Compare the population of two cities _____

2. Show the change in population of two cities from 2000–2005 _____

3. Compare the cost of long distance phone calls from 1950–2000 _____

4. Compare the average height of students in two classes _____

Thinking About Double-Bar and Line Graphs and Coordinate Grids

The information from double line graphs can easily be displayed on a coordinate grid. The information for each line is given as coordinates on the grid. Look at the information presented below about the percentage of households using landlines and cell phones. To translate this onto a coordinate grid, the x-axis is marked in years. Let 1990 correspond to 0, 1991 to 1, and so on. Therefore, 2004 corresponds to 14. The y-axis is marked in percent from 0 to 100. Let each unit on the axis represent 5 percent. The line representing landlines has coordinates (0, 11) and (14, 12). The line representing cell phones has coordinates $(0, \frac{2}{5})$ and $(14, 12\frac{2}{5})$. Notice that 62 percent is $\frac{2}{5}$ of the distance between 60 percent and 65 percent.

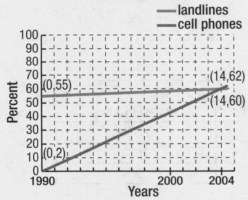

Percent of Households Using Landlines and Cell Phones

1. Does the graph indicate an increase in the percent of households using landline phones?

   _____

2. What is the increase in the percent of households using cell phones?

   _____

3. Describe the two lines on the graph at 2004.

   _____

4. How would you compare the use of landline phones and cell phones after 2004?

   _____

   _____

Show That You Know

Read the information below. Use what you read about addition and multiplication to answer the questions. Remember what you have learned in this lesson about multiplication. Use the space provided to show your work.

Shelby is going to report to her class on the daily internet activities of both broadband users and dial-up users. She recorded the results of her research in the chart below and needs to make a decision about what type of graph will best represent her information.

Recall the types of graphs you learned in Unit 1.

Internet Users		
	Broadband Users	**Dial-Up Users**
News	41%	23%
Research for work	30%	15%
Download Music	13%	3%

1. What type of graph compares changes over time?

2. What type of graph compares quantities?

3. What type of graph should Shelby use to best represent her data? Explain your choice.

4. What should the vertical scale on her graph represent?

5. How can she represent 41 percent on the scale?

Show That You Know *(continued)*

6. How should she label the *x*-axis?

7. Which bar represents the greatest amount?

8. Which bar represents the least amount?

9. Which Internet activity shows the greatest difference

between broadband and dial-up?

10. Construct the graph.

Review What You've Learned

11. What have you learned in this Connections lesson about the differences in bar graphs, line
graphs, and coordinate graphs?

12. What have you learned in this Connections lesson that you did not already know?

13. What have you learned in this lesson that will help you read or construct bar, line, and coordinate
graphs?

Review and Practice

Skills Review

Decimals:

Decimals are numbers that include parts of a whole. The digits on the right side of the decimal point represent the parts of a whole.

Fifty and seven tenths: 50.7

Three and nineteen hundredths: 3.19

Working with multidigit numbers:

One way to add or subtract large numbers is to line up the place values vertically. Work right to left and carry or regroup as needed.

$$\begin{array}{r} 38 \\ -\ 15 \\ \hline 23 \end{array} \qquad \begin{array}{r} 55 \\ +\ 22 \\ \hline 77 \end{array}$$

Adding decimals:

To add decimals, line up the decimal points and the place values vertically.

$$\begin{array}{r} 3.89 \\ +\ 1.01 \\ \hline 4.90 \end{array}$$

Subtracting decimals:

To subtract decimals, line up the decimal points and the place values vertically.

$$\begin{array}{r} 5.22 \\ -\ 3.15 \\ \hline 2.07 \end{array}$$

Estimating decimal sums and differences:

Use rounding to estimate sums and differences of decimals.

For $0.62 + 0.89$, 0.62 rounds to 0.6 and 0.89 rounds to 0.9.

$0.6 + 0.9 = 1.5$; So, $0.62 + 0.89$ is about 1.5.

$0.86 - 0.22 \rightarrow 0.9 - 0.2 = 0.7$

Estimating fraction sums and differences:

Changing the numerator or denominator to a compatible number can help round fractions. The simplified fraction can then be changed to a decimal.

$\frac{3}{8} + 0.6 \rightarrow \frac{4}{8} + 0.6 \rightarrow \frac{1}{2} + 0.6 \rightarrow 0.5 + 0.6 = 1.1$

Strategy Review

- Make initial estimates of solutions to addition problems involving money. The actual answer should be close to the estimate.

- Also make estimates of solutions to subtraction problems involving money.

Skills and Strategies Practice

Complete the exercises below.

1. $11.3 + 3.4 =$ _____

4. $19.7 + 2.32 =$ _____

2. Make an estimate of the sum of $2.03 and $100.99.

_____

5. Round these numbers to the nearest tenth and estimate the difference: $6.01 - 4.23$

_____

_____

3. $17.56 - 17.2 =$ _____

6. Use rounding to estimate the sum of $\frac{8}{36} + 0.9$.

_____

_____

TEST-TAKING tip

Always look for decimals in the numbers you are given in a problem and check your placement of the decimal point in your answer. As an example, $3.3 - 3.3$ is a different problem than $33 - 3.3$, even though the digits are the same. $3.3 - 3.3 = 0$, while $33 - 3.3 = 26.7$. It may help you to say the numbers in your head, such as *thirty-three and three-tenths* minus *three and three-tenths* as a way of keeping track of the decimal point.

Unit Review

Circle the letter of the correct answer.

1. $9.1 + 3.77 =$ _____

    A. 12.77   C. 36.8

    B. 12.87   D. 12.78

2. $8.7 - 5.2 =$ _____

    A. 3.5   C. 5.3

    B. 13.9   D. 3.7

3. Estimate the sum $0.887 + 0.334$.

    A. 1.4   C. 1.2

    B. 1.0   D. 1.1

4. $61.1 + 0.33 =$ _____

    A. 64.4   C. 61.43

    B. 61.44   D. 61.34

5. $50 - 1.1 =$ _____

    A. 39   C. 49.9

    B. 39.9   D. 48.9

6. Estimate $\frac{2}{7} + 1.4$.

    A. 1.8   C. 1.55

    B. 1.65   D. 1.45

7. $6.6 + 2.3 =$ _____

    A. 8.9   C. 4.3

    B. 9.8   D. 8.3

8. $8.3 - 1.5 =$ _____

    A. 9.8   C. 6.8

    B. 7.8   D. 5.8

9. $3.4 + 4.3 =$ _____

    A. 7.9   C. 7.4

    B. 7.7   D. 0.9

10. A reasonable estimate of $1.27 - 1.01$ is _____.

    A. 0.1   C. 2.3

    B. 0.3   D. 1.3

11. 10.3434 rounded to the nearest tenth is _____.

    A. 10.3   C. 10.34

    B. 10.4   D. 10.35

12. $16.8 - 9.1 =$ _____

    A. 8.7   C. 158.9

    B. 25.9   D. 7.7

13. Estimate $\frac{8}{9} - 0.6$.

    A. 1.6   C. 0.3

    B. 0.4   D. 0.1

14. $1.1 + 4.5 =$ _____

    A. 5.6   C. 3.4

    B. 5.5   D. 5.7

15. 89.1 − 89.05 = _____

   A. 0.4   C. 0.05

   B. 0.5   D. 0.6

16. A reasonable estimate of $\frac{5}{16}$ + 0.1 is _____.

   A. 0.65   C. 0.35

   B. 0.45   D. 0.25

17. 3.13 + 0.2 = _____

   A. 3.15   C. 3.23

   B. 3.33   D. 3.25

18. 9.89 rounded to the nearest tenth is _____.

   A. 9.99   C. 10

   B. 9.8   D. 9.9

19. 7.7 − 6.2 = _____

   A. 0.5   C. 1.4

   B. 0.05   D. 1.5

20. Estimate 7.113 + 8.222.

   A. 15.3   C. 15.2

   B. 1.1   D. 15.4

21. 17.1 + 3.2 = _____

   A. 13.9   C. 20.3

   B. 21.3   D. 19.4

22. A good estimate of $\frac{15}{14}$ − 1 is _____.

   A. 2   C. 0

   B. 1   D. $\frac{13}{14}$

23. 11.1 − 1.1 = _____

   A. 0   C. 12.2

   B. 10   D. 0.1

24. 1.92 − 0.47 = _____

   A. 0   C. 1.4

   B. 1.45   D. 0.45

25. 1.6 + 2.4 = _____

   A. 4   C. 8.5

   B. 3.9   D. 5.8

26. Estimate 13.491 − 2.120.

   A. 12.4   C. 11.9

   B. 12.3   D. 11.4

27. 6.1 − 5.2 = _____

   A. 1.2   C. 0.9

   B. 1.9   D. 0.8

28. 1.4 + 1.5 = _____

   A. 1.9   C. 2.0

   B. 1.09   D. 2.9

Unit 3 Reflection

MATH SKILLS

The easiest part about adding and subtracting decimals is

Reciprocals are useful because

Communication and Technology

MATH STRATEGIES & CONNECTIONS

For me, the math strategies that work the best are

Expressing fractions as decimals is useful when

READING STRATEGIES & COMPREHENSION

The easiest part about questioning is

One way that questioning helps me with reading is

The vocabulary words I had trouble with are

INDEPENDENT READING

My favorite part of <u>Communication and Technology</u> is

I read most fluently when

UNIT 4
Multiplication and Division of Fractions and Decimals

MATH SKILLS & STRATEGIES
After you learn the basic **SKILLS**, the real test is knowing when to use each **STRATEGY.**

AMP LINK MAGAZINE
You Do the Math and Math Projects: After you read each magazine article, apply what you know in real-world problems. Fluency: Make your reading smooth and accurate, one tip at a time.

READING STRATEGY
Learn the power of Previewing and Predicting.

CONNECTIONS
You own the math when you make your own connections.

VOCABULARY
MATH WORDS:
Know them!
Use them!
Learn all about them!

Reading Comprehension Strategy: Previewing/Predicting

How to Preview and Predict

Preview the article by reading the **title** and **subtitles**.	Look at the **photos.** Read the **captions.**	Think about **what you already know** about the topic or related topics.	Now **predict** what you think the article is about. What will you learn about as you read?	As you read, use what you learn to **check your prediction.** You may change it at any time.

To **preview,** you look through the pages you are going to read. Read the **title, subtitles,** and **captions.** Study the **photos.** Look at the last paragraph of the article to see how it ends. Are there review questions? They can tell you what you should look for while reading. When you preview, also look for **bold** words.

10,000 Steps

How far is 10,000 steps? One step for the average person is about 2.5 feet. Do the math, and you will see that it takes about 2,000 steps to go 1 mile. So 10,000 steps is about five miles. Do you think you walk five miles in one day? Everyone should try to take 10,000 steps each day to stay strong and healthy.

1. What do the title and subtitles tell you about the subject of the article?

_____

_____

_____

Before you read, look at photos and read their captions. Use what you see and read to **predict** something about the article. Try to add to your prediction by using details from the photos.

How To Count Your Steps

The best way to find out how many steps you take is to wear a pedometer. A pedometer is a small machine that counts each step you take. It senses each time you lift a foot and then put it down again. At the end of the day, you check the pedometer to find out how many steps you took.

2. What do you already know about the information in this paragraph? How did this help you as you read?

_____

_____

_____

_____

_____

_____

_____

_____

You have previewed the text and made predictions based on titles, subtitles, and photos. Before you read, think about **what you already know** about the topic. You can use your knowledge and experience to predict what the article will tell you.

How To Make Your Steps Count

Did you know that there is a right way (and many wrong ways) to walk for exercise? Both the right and wrong ways will get you to where you want to be. However, only the right way will help you strengthen your body at the same time. Avoid these common walking mistakes.

3. Make a prediction about what you will learn about walking and walking mistakes.

_____

_____

Now you are ready to read the whole article. As you read, check the predictions you have made. Make new predictions as you read. Check them as you learn more.

First, stand up straight. Leaning forward may cause shoulder, neck, and back pain. Next, take small, quick steps, rather than long strides. Long strides can hurt your shins, making it painful to walk at all. Then, swing your arms naturally to help you move gracefully. Finally, hit the ground with the heel of your foot and then roll forward, Try not to "slap" the ground with your foot.

4. What did you think you would learn from this passage? Was your prediction accurate?

_____

_____

_____

_____

When you **predict,** you make smart guesses about what an article will tell you. You add your knowledge and experience to what you read to **make and check predictions.** Making predictions helps you understand and remember more of what you read.

Walk Into Your Future!

You will find many ways to add steps to your day. You can walk your dog—or walk someone else's dog. You can take the stairs rather than an elevator. You can mow the lawn or walk to the park to hang out with friends. You can walk around your block while text messaging your friends. No matter how you do it, try to add a few more steps every day. Before you know it, your pedometer will read 10,000. Better yet, you will get stronger every day!

5. Look at the predictions you have made so far. Were you right? How can you add to or change your prediction so that it is correct?

_____

_____

_____

_____

_____

6. What is the most useful strategy for predicting? Explain your answer.

_____

_____

_____

Use the Strategies

Use the reading comprehension strategies you have learned to answer questions about the article below.

Let It Snow!

Snow Surfing

Winter sports are those that involve snow and ice. In recent decades, snowboarding has emerged as one of the most popular winter sports. The idea for the first snowboard was born in Michigan when a man saw his children sliding downhill on sleds—standing up. He fastened two skis together and let the children "surf" downhill sideways. Modern snowboards are made of layered wood and fiberglass. A snowboard's style depends on how the rider wants to use it.

Downhill Racers

One popular type of snowboarding is called Alpine snowboarding. The word Alpine refers to anything that happens in the mountains. Alpine riders use a hard, narrow board for easy downhill cruises or to speed down snowy mountainsides. One part of Alpine riding is racing. Every year, there are numerous competitive races for Alpine snowboarders. There is even an Olympic race called the "giant slalom."

A Borrowed Style

Freestyle snowboarding is very much like skateboarding in the snow. Freestyle riders use shorter, more flexible boards. They practice tricks and jumps that are borrowed from skateboarders. Freestyle snowboarding also includes many of the same "urban" elements and obstacles in their tricks. Boxes, handrails, and small ramps are built in the snow for freestyle riders to perform tricks. For competitions, huge ramps called half-pipes are built in the snow. Riders go back and forth on the ramps, picking up speeds that send them high above the "lip" of the ramp.

1. Based on the title and subtitles, what might this article be about?

_____

_____

_____

2. How can you preview the information on this page?

_____

_____

_____

3. After you have previewed the page, make a prediction about what the article is about. Write your prediction below.

_____

_____

_____

4. What goal-setting question could you ask about the last paragraph? Write an answer to your question.

_____

_____

_____

5. Summarize the last paragraph in one sentence.

_____

_____

_____

_____

Reading Strategies: Summarizing, Questioning, Previewing/Predicting

Use the reading comprehension strategies you have learned in the previous units to answer the questions below.

1. How do the subheadings help you figure out what the article is about?

   _____

   _____

2. What knowledge did you already have about snowboarding before you read this article? How did it help you understand what you read?

   _____

   _____

3. Write a question that you still have about this article. Reread the article and answer your question.

   _____

   _____

4. Write a summary for the whole article.

   _____

   _____

   _____

   _____

Problem-Solving Strategies:
Draw a Picture or Use a Model, Find a Pattern, Make a List

Use the problem-solving strategies you have learned in the previous units to answer the questions below.

5. How could making a list help you better understand the article about snowboarding?

   _____

   _____

6. In a snowboard shop, boards are four different lengths: 215 cm, 190 cm, 165 cm, and 140 cm. What is the rule for the pattern these numbers make?

   _____

   _____

7. Draw a picture of a snowboard based on the first paragraph. How does drawing the snowboard help you better understand what you have read?

   _____

   _____

Multiplying Fractions

Learn the SKILL

Katie ordered a pizza with mushrooms and anchovies as toppings. When she received the pizza, only five out of eight slices had mushrooms on them. Half of the slices with mushrooms also had anchovies. What fraction of the entire pizza had both mushrooms and anchovies?

SKILL	EXAMPLE	COMPLETE THE EXAMPLE
You can calculate a fraction of a fraction by finding the product of the two fractions. To multiply two fractions, find the product of the numerators and then the product of the denominators. If possible, simplify the product.	Multiply $\frac{5}{8} \times \frac{1}{2}$. $\frac{5}{8} \times \frac{1}{2} = \frac{5 \times 1}{8 \times 2} = \frac{5}{16}$ The only common factor of 5 and 16 is one, so $\frac{5}{16}$ is already written in simplest form.	Multiply $\frac{2}{3} \times \frac{3}{4}$. _____
	Multiply $\frac{4}{3} \times \frac{3}{4}$. $\frac{4}{3} \times \frac{3}{4} = \frac{4 \times 3}{3 \times 4} = \frac{12}{12} = 1$	Multiply $\frac{6}{5} \times \frac{1}{2}$. _____

Use what you already know about adding and subtracting fractions, to help you solve.

Choose the Right Word

> denominator   simplify   fraction
> improper fraction

Fill each blank with the correct word or phrase from the box.

1. A(n) _____ is part of a whole.

2. The _____ is the bottom part of the fraction.

3. To _____ is to rewrite an expression or fraction in its simplest form.

4. In a(n) _____ the numerator is greater than or equal to the denominator.

Yes or No?

Answer these questions and be ready to explain your answers.

5. Do the denominators have to be equal in order to multiply two fractions? _____

6. Is the denominator larger than the numerator in an improper fraction? _____

7. Can the fraction $\frac{4}{12}$ be simplified? _____

8. Is it possible that the product of two fractions would be able to be simplified? _____

Show That You Know

Multiply the fractions. Simplify if possible.

9. $\frac{1}{3} \times \frac{3}{4} =$

10. $\frac{4}{3} \times \frac{5}{6} =$

11. $\frac{2}{5} \times \frac{6}{1} =$

12. $\frac{1}{3} \times \frac{1}{3} =$

13. $\frac{7}{2} \times \frac{1}{3} =$

14. $\frac{11}{4} \times \frac{3}{2} =$

15. $\frac{5}{4} \times \frac{1}{10} =$

SOLVE on Your Own

Skills Practice

Now that you know about multiplying fractions, show it by solving these problems!

Multiply the fractions. Simplify if possible.

1. $\frac{2}{3} \times \frac{3}{2} =$ _____

2. $\frac{4}{5} \times \frac{1}{4} =$ _____

3. $\frac{3}{2} \times \frac{6}{7} =$ _____

4. $\frac{1}{3} \times \frac{1}{2} =$ _____

5. $\frac{1}{4} \times \frac{24}{6} =$ _____

6. $\frac{3}{5} \times \frac{1}{5} =$ _____

7. $\frac{3}{3} \times \frac{1}{3} =$ _____

8. $\frac{9}{2} \times \frac{2}{4} =$ _____

9. $\frac{5}{2} \times \frac{3}{5} =$ _____

10. $\frac{2}{5} \times \frac{4}{5} =$ _____

11. $\frac{1}{5} \times \frac{10}{3} =$ _____

12. $\frac{5}{4} \times \frac{2}{7} =$ _____

Multiplying Fractions
Strategy
Draw a Picture or Use a Model

Step 1: Read At Central Junior High, $\frac{2}{3}$ of the school's students are cheerleaders, and $\frac{1}{4}$ of the cheerleaders are male. What fraction of the school's students are male cheerleaders?

STRATEGY	SOLUTION
Draw a Picture or Use a Model You can use a model to help you multiply fractions. First, divide a rectangle into equal columns and color the columns to show the first fraction. Then, divide the rectangle into equal rows and fill in the rows with a different color to show the second fraction. The part of the rectangle where the colors overlap represents the product of the two fractions.	Step 2: Plan Make a model to find $\frac{2}{3} \times \frac{1}{4}$. Step 3: Solve To model $\frac{2}{3}$, divide a rectangle into three equal columns and color the first two.  Then divide the rectangle into four equal rows and color the first row blue to show $\frac{1}{4}$.  Two of the 12 equal parts are colored both blue and red, so $\frac{2}{12}$ or $\frac{1}{6}$ in simplest form, of the school's students are male cheerleaders. Step 4: Check Check $\frac{2}{3} \times \frac{1}{4} = \frac{(2 \times 1)}{(3 \times 4)} = \frac{2}{12} = \frac{1}{6}$

Read the problem several times before you start to draw your picture or use a model.

YOUR TURN

Choose the Right Word

denominator   numerator
simplest form   simplify

Fill in each blank with the correct word or phrase from the box.

1. To _____ a fraction, you must rewrite it in its _____.

2. In the fraction $\frac{3}{4}$, the _____ is three.

3. The number below the line in a fraction is called the _____.

Yes or No?

Answer these questions and be ready to explain your answers.

4. When using a model to multiply fractions, is the product shown by all of the colored parts? _____

5. When you multiply fractions, is the product always in simplest form? _____

6. Does a product of two fractions always need to be simplified? _____

7. Can you multiply improper fractions? _____

8. Can you ever simplify fractions before multiplying them? _____

Show That You Know

Multiply the fractions. Write your answers in simplest form.

9. $\frac{3}{4} \times \frac{6}{7}$

10. $\frac{5}{8} \times \frac{7}{5}$

11. $\frac{11}{8} \times \frac{5}{4}$

12. $\frac{2}{5} \times \frac{25}{7}$

13. $\frac{9}{10} \times \frac{25}{18}$

Solve these word problems by multiplying fractions. Put your answers in simplest form.

14. Two-thirds of the voters were in favor of the bill. Of those voters in favor of the bill, $\frac{1}{2}$ were women. What fraction of the voters were women in favor of the bill?

15. Of the people in line for the movie, $\frac{4}{5}$ were under the age of 12. Of those, $\frac{5}{7}$ had seen the movie once already. What fraction of the people in line were under the age of 12 and had seen the movie already?

READ on Your Own

Reading Comprehension Strategy: Previewing/Predicting

Intense Sports, *pages 3–5*

VOCABULARY

Watch for the words you are learning about.

cheerleaders: athletes who perform athletic stunts aimed at leading a crowd in rooting for a team

intense sport: an extreme or exciting physical activity that may be more dangerous than other sports

Fluency Tip

Keep a pace that holds interest. Tell events as if you were part of them.

Before You Read

Think about the last time you were at a football or basketball game. Were there cheerleaders at the game? Did you feel the cheerleaders made the game more fun? Why or why not?

As You Read

Preview by reading the first paragraph of "Good Cheer,"

page 3.

In the chart below, write a prediction of what you think the reading will be about. Be sure to elaborate on your prediction with some details.

Read "Good Cheer," pages 3–4.

Answer the question in the right column of the chart.

Good Cheer	
Prediction: _____ _____ _____ _____	Did your prediction match what you read about or was there information in the text that you did not expect? Explain. _____ _____ _____

After You Read

Do you think that schools should ban dangerous cheerleading stunts or make rules about how and when they are performed? Why or why not?

_____

_____

SOLVE on Your Own

Intense Sports, *page 5*

Organize the Information

Read You Do the Math in the magazine.
Then complete the table below.

Putting information in a table will help you answer these questions.

Length of Routine	Pyramid Formation	Falling Pyramid	Flip Stunts	Dance Routines
5 min	$1\frac{2}{3}$ min			

You Do the Math

Use the information in the table to help you answer the questions. You may answer the questions on a piece of paper or in the space provided below. Remember to use the Four-Step Problem-Solving Plan.

1. How could you use addition of fractions to check your answers in the table above?

_____

_____

2. How could you use the fractions from the competition rules to choose easy lengths to work with?

_____

_____

_____

After You Solve

How else could you display the information in the table above?

_____

_____

Dividing Fractions

Learn the SKILL

There were $\frac{3}{7}$ of the students in Rob's school that went on a field trip. The teachers divided the students on the trip into six smaller groups for activities. What fraction of the total students in the school were in each group?

SKILL	EXAMPLE	COMPLETE THE EXAMPLE
The first step to dividing fractions is to find the **reciprocal** of the second fraction. To find the reciprocal, the fraction must be **inverted.**	Find the reciprocal of $\frac{2}{5}$. $\frac{2}{5}$ inverted $= \frac{5}{2}$	Find the reciprocal of $\frac{3}{4}$. _____
To divide both proper and improper fractions, the reciprocal of the second fraction is multiplied by the first fraction.	Divide $\frac{3}{5} \div \frac{2}{5}$. $\frac{3}{5} \times \frac{5}{2}$ $\frac{3}{5} \times \frac{5}{2} = \frac{15}{10} = \frac{3}{2} = 1\frac{1}{2}$	Divide $\frac{4}{3} \div \frac{2}{1}$. _____
To divide a fraction by a whole number, first rewrite the whole number as a fraction by writing a one for the denominator. Then follow the above steps for dividing fractions.	Divide $\frac{3}{7} \div 6$. 6 can be rewritten as $\frac{6}{1}$, so the reciprocal is $\frac{1}{6}$. $\frac{3}{7} \times \frac{1}{6} = \frac{3}{42} = \frac{1}{14}$ So, $\frac{3}{7} \div 6 = \frac{1}{14}$	Divide $\frac{4}{7} \div 5$. _____

YOUR TURN

Choose the Right Word

> invert   improper fraction
> reciprocal   simplify

Fill each blank with the correct word or phrase from the box.

1. To _____ is to replace an expression with its simplest form.

2. The product of a number, multiplied by its _____, is one.

3. $\frac{5}{5}$ is an example of a(n) _____, but $\frac{3}{5}$ is not.

4. To reverse the positions of the numerator and denominator is to _____ a fraction.

Yes or No?

Answer these questions and be ready to explain your answers.

5. Can a fraction be divided by an improper fraction? _____

6. Is the first fraction (the dividend) inverted when dividing fractions? _____

7. Should both fractions be inverted to divide the fractions? _____

8. Does multiplying a fraction by its reciprocal always equal one? _____

Show That You Know

Find the reciprocal.

9. $\frac{3}{5} =$

10. $\frac{2}{3} =$

11. $\frac{4}{11} =$

12. $\frac{2}{9} =$

13. $\frac{7}{4} =$

Divide. Simplify if possible.

14. $\frac{2}{3} \div \frac{1}{3} =$

15. $\frac{3}{8} \div \frac{1}{7} =$

16. $\frac{1}{4} \div \frac{2}{3} =$

17. $\frac{3}{5} \div \frac{6}{7} =$

18. $\frac{2}{9} \div 4 =$

SOLVE on Your Own

Skills Practice

Find the reciprocal in its simplest form.

Remember, to find the reciprocal, invert the fraction. The reciprocal of a whole number is one divided by the number.

1. $\frac{1}{4}$ _____

2. $\frac{7}{3}$ _____

3. $\frac{2}{4}$ _____

4. 6 _____

5. $\frac{6}{3}$ _____

Divide. Simplify if possible.

6. $\frac{4}{5} \div \frac{5}{4}$ _____

7. $\frac{3}{7} \div \frac{7}{4}$ _____

8. $\frac{9}{2} \div \frac{1}{9}$ _____

9. $\frac{5}{2} \div \frac{10}{3}$ _____

10. $\frac{2}{5} \div \frac{1}{2}$ _____

11. $\frac{4}{3} \div \frac{3}{4}$ _____

12. $\frac{2}{5} \div \frac{3}{4}$ _____

13. $\frac{3}{4} \div \frac{1}{2}$ _____

14. $\frac{4}{5} \div \frac{3}{8}$ _____

15. $\frac{2}{7} \div 9$ _____

Dividing Fractions

Strategy

Try a Simpler Form of the Problem

Step 1: Read Marcus is fast and loves to run. Today he is running in a race with over 1,000 people. Marcus has run $\frac{3}{5}$ of the race so far. He has run $\frac{5}{4}$ miles. How long is the entire race?

STRATEGY	SOLUTION
Try a Simpler Form of the Problem To see how to solve a problem, you can change the numbers or fractions in a problem to numbers or fractions that are easier to work with. Using a simpler form of the problem can help you see how to solve it. Remember to switch back to the original numbers to find the solution.	**Step 2: Plan** Restate the problem with simpler numbers, such as $\frac{1}{2}$. Then go back to the original fractions. **Step 3: Solve** Instead of the given fractions, suppose the problem said Marcus has run $\frac{1}{2}$ of the race and that he has run 1 mile. This means $\frac{1}{2}$ of the entire race is 1 mile, so the whole race is 2 miles. You can get this result by dividing 1 by $\frac{1}{2}$: $1 \div \frac{1}{2} = \frac{1}{1} \div \frac{1}{2} = \frac{1}{1} \times \frac{2}{1} = \frac{2}{1} = 2$ Now, do the same thing using the original numbers. The distance Marcus has run is $\frac{5}{4}$ miles. So divide this distance by $\frac{3}{5}$. To divide by $\frac{3}{5}$, you multiply by the reciprocal, $\frac{5}{3}$. $\frac{5}{4} \div \frac{3}{5} = \frac{5}{4} \times \frac{5}{3} = \frac{25}{12}$ In this case the fraction does not simplify. The entire race is $\frac{25}{12}$ miles. (You can change this to a mixed number: $2\frac{1}{12}$ miles.) **Step 4: Check** Multiply the quotient by the divisor and then simplify to check the answer. $\frac{3}{5} \times \frac{25}{12} = \frac{75}{60} = \frac{75 \div 15}{60 \div 15} = \frac{5}{4}$

Start by solving the problem with easier numbers. Remember each step as you solve. Then go back and plug in the original numbers to get the answer to the problem.

YOUR TURN

Choose the Right Word

dividend   divisor   invert   reciprocal

Fill in each blank with the correct word or phrase from the box.

1. The whole number four has a _____ that looks like $\frac{1}{4}$.

2. In a division expression, the _____ is divided by the _____.

3. To _____ a fraction, you reverse the position of the numerator and denominator.

Yes or No?

Answer these questions and be ready to explain your answers.

4. Can changing to simpler numbers in a word problem help you to solve it? _____

5. When you divide fractions, does it matter in which order you divide them? _____

6. When you divide fractions, is it always possible to simplify the quotient? _____

7. Can you divide improper fractions? _____

8. Can you ever simplify fractions before dividing them? _____

Show That You Know

Divide the fractions. Put your answers in simplest form.

9. $\frac{2}{3} \div \frac{2}{5} =$

10. $\frac{9}{4} \div \frac{5}{4} =$

11. $\frac{13}{3} \div \frac{2}{9} =$

12. $\frac{8}{7} \div \frac{2}{11} =$

13. $\frac{12}{7} \div \frac{22}{9} =$

Divide the fractions. Put your answers in simplest form.

14. Dannika swam $\frac{3}{4}$ of the distance she needs to swim for today's practice. She has swum $\frac{9}{2}$ laps so far. How many laps does Dannika need to swim for today's practice?

15. Mo has completed $\frac{1}{3}$ of the pages he needs to write for his term paper. He has written $\frac{11}{3}$ pages so far. How many pages long does Mo's term paper need to be?

READ on Your Own

Reading Comprehension Strategy: Previewing/Predicting

Intense Sports, *pages 6–8*

VOCABULARY

Watch for the words you are learning about.

BASE jumping: the sport of jumping off a non-moving object with a parachute

skydiving: the sport of jumping out of an airplane with a parachute

Fluency Tip

Notice changes in the author's tone and match it with the expression in your voice.

Before You Read

Recall what you read about in "Good Cheer." Why would a toss stunt be dangerous?

As You Read

Look through the text features in order to preview "Skydiving: A Sport to Fall For," pages 6–8. STOP

Write a prediction for what you think "Skydiving: A Sport to Fall For" will be about. Be sure to be detailed about your prediction.

_____

_____

_____

Now read "Skydiving: A Sport to Fall For," pages 6–8. STOP

Did giving details in your prediction help you to better understand the text? Explain.

_____

_____

_____

After You Read

Have you ever seen or touched a parachute up close? What was the material like, or what do you think it would feel like?

_____

_____

_____

SOLVE on Your Own

Intense Sports, *page 8*

Organize the Information

Putting the key information in a table will help you answer the magazine questions.

Read You Do the Math in the magazine. Then complete the table below.

	Distance Before Parachute Opened	Fraction of Jump Before Parachute Opened	Height of Jump
Miss Patel	400 ft	$\frac{2}{5}$	
Kayla	470 ft	$\frac{1}{2}$	
Hector	340 ft	$\frac{2}{7}$	
Marcus	318 ft	$\frac{3}{8}$	
Nadia	315 ft	$\frac{3}{7}$	
Todd	180 ft	$\frac{1}{5}$	

You Do the Math

Use the information in the table above to answer these questions. Write your answers in the space provided.

1. Which operation did you use to find the height of each jump? How did you know which operation to use?

   _____

   _____

   _____

2. Which jumpers traveled the greatest and shortest total distances? Which of these was a more dangerous jump? Explain.

   _____

   _____

After You Solve

Would you ever want to go skydiving or BASE jumping? Why or why not?

_____

The Four-Step Problem-Solving Plan

Step 1: Read	Step 2: Plan	Step 3: Solve	Step 4: Check
Make sure you understand what the problem is asking.	Decide how you will solve the problem.	Solve the problem using your plan.	Check to make sure your answer is correct.

Read the article below. Then answer the questions.

That's a Goal!

Ice hockey is an old game. The first game of ice hockey took place in 1875 in Canada.

In hockey, the primary goal is to get the puck, a hard rubber disk roughly the size of your palm, into your opponent's net. The entire game is played on an ice rink, which is typically surrounded by a wall and tall, clear plastic shields. The game is divided into three periods, each lasting 20 minutes.

Typically there are five players and a goalie on the ice for each team. Play is very physical. Players must wear nine different pieces of protective gear—more gear than in football. Breaking the rules and injuring another player results in a penalty. A regular penalty puts the player who broke the rule or injured another player in the penalty box for $\frac{1}{10}$ of a period. Double penalties last $\frac{1}{5}$ of a period, and a really serious offense, or attack, results in a penalty that is $\frac{1}{4}$ of a period. During this time, the other team has more players on the ice. This is known as a power play and adds excitement to the game.

1. If a player has been in the penalty box for $\frac{2}{3}$ of a double penalty, for what fraction of the period has their penalty lasted so far? Show your work.

_____

_____

2. According to the article, what equipment do you need to play hockey?

_____

_____

_____

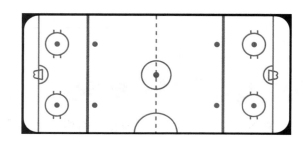

Read the article below. Then answer the questions.

Shop and Swap

In many intense or extreme sports, special equipment is needed. Unfortunately, for athletes on a budget, it is just not safe to buy cheaply made, less durable equipment. But that does not mean you have to spend all your money to be sure you have the right equipment. You can stay safe by shopping carefully.

One way to save money is to buy last year's model. Stores usually mark down what was last year's latest, greatest equipment in order to make room for this year's new thing. Another way to save money is to buy gently used equipment. For example, many ski shops host a "swap" in the fall. At these events, individuals bring the equipment they outgrew or will not need any more and sell it for less than they paid for it brand new.

As thrifty as you may be, there are some things you would not want to buy used. You want to avoid buying used safety equipment such as helmets because it is impossible to know what they have been through. Take the money you saved on a used pair of ski boots and buy a new ski helmet.

1. Ali bought a pair of skis. The skis were $\frac{2}{5}$ of their original price. If she paid $100 for the skis, how much did they originally cost? (Hint: Try using simpler numbers to find how to solve the problem.)

_____

_____

2. What advice does the author give for buying sports equipment?

_____

_____

_____

Fluency Tip

Use emotion as you read. Emphasize the main ideas and important details by changing the tone of your voice.

READ on Your Own

Reading Comprehension Strategy: Previewing/Predicting

Intense Sports, *pages 9–11*

Before You Read

Consider the sport of skydiving that you read about in "Skydiving: A Sport to Fall For." What would appeal to people about this sport?

As You Read

Preview "Curling, Bowling, and Bocce," pages 9–11.

Write your prediction below.

Read "Curling, Bowling, and Bocce," pages 9–11.

Fill in the remaining information.

What I predict:

_____

_____

Information in the article I predicted:

_____

_____

Information in the article that I did not predict:

_____

_____

After You Read

How does previewing help you better understand the article? Explain your answer.

_____

_____

VOCABULARY

Watch for the words you are learning about.

bocce: an Italian lawn game in which players try to throw their balls closest to a target ball

curling: a game in which two teams of four players each slide heavy stones over ice toward a target circle

Fluency Tip

Use punctuation marks to help you read long sentences. Give a short pause for a comma and a longer pause for a period.

SOLVE on Your Own

Intense Sports, *page 12*

Organize the Information

Use the diagram below to organize the information you find in the Math Project on magazine page 12.

Friends   **Going to competition**

The "of" in "$\frac{1}{3}$ of $\frac{1}{2}$" means "multiply."

Math Project

Use the information in the diagram above to answer these questions. Write your answers in the space provided.

1. If you drew a picture to solve the problem, how did you represent the total number of friends? If you did not draw a picture, what strategy did you use to solve the problem?

_____

_____

_____

_____

2. What did you do if you ended up with a mixed fraction as an answer? Why?

_____

After You Solve

How could you express the same information in an equation?

_____

_____

Multiplying and Dividing Mixed Numbers

Learn the SKILL

Sammy and his friend Shawn met at the park for soccer practice. They each rode their bikes from their homes to the park. Sammy rode his bike $4\frac{1}{2}$ miles. His friend Shawn only rode $\frac{2}{3}$ of the distance Sammy rode. How far did Shawn ride?

VOCABULARY

Watch for the words you are learning about.

convert: to change from one form to another

SKILL	EXAMPLE	COMPLETE THE EXAMPLE
The first step to multiplying or dividing with mixed numbers is to change them into improper fractions by multiplying the whole part by the denominator and adding the product to the numerator. Remember to simplify if possible.	Change to an improper fraction. $4\frac{1}{2}$ $4 \times 2 + 1 = 9$ $4\frac{1}{2} = \frac{9}{2}$	Rewrite $2\frac{3}{4}$ as an improper fraction. _____
After the mixed numbers have been **converted** to improper fractions, then the two fractions can be multiplied.	Find $\frac{2}{3}$ of $4\frac{1}{2}$ miles. $\frac{2}{3} \times 4\frac{1}{2} = \frac{2}{3} \times \frac{9}{2}$ $= \frac{(2 \times 9)}{(3 \times 2)} = \frac{18}{6}$ Simplify if possible. $\frac{18}{6} = \frac{3}{1} = 3$ $\frac{2}{3}$ of $4\frac{1}{2}$ miles is 3 miles.	Multiply $2\frac{3}{4} \times 1\frac{1}{4}$. _____
Mixed numbers can also be divided after they have been converted to improper fractions.	Divide $3\frac{1}{3} \div \frac{3}{7}$. $3\frac{1}{3} = \frac{10}{3}$ $\frac{10}{3} \div \frac{3}{7} = \frac{10}{3} \times \frac{7}{3} = \frac{70}{9}$ or $7\frac{7}{9}$	Divide $2\frac{3}{4} \div 1\frac{1}{4}$. _____

YOUR TURN

Choose the Right Word

> convert   improper fraction
> mixed number   simplify

Fill in each blank with the correct word or phrase from the box.

1. To _____ is to replace a fraction with its simplest form.

2. A(n) _____ is a number with a whole number part and a fractional part.

3. To _____ a number is to change it from one form into another.

4. An example of a(n) _____ is $\frac{13}{8}$.

Yes or No?

Answer these questions and be ready to explain your answers.

5. Can a mixed number be multiplied by a whole number? _____

6. Can a mixed number be divided by a proper fraction? _____

7. Can a mixed number be divided by zero? _____

8. Does an improper fraction need to be converted to a mixed number before multiplying? _____

Show That You Know

Convert to an improper fraction.

9. $2\frac{3}{5}$

10. $6\frac{2}{3}$

11. $1\frac{2}{5}$

Divide. Simplify if possible.

12. $2\frac{2}{3} \div 3\frac{1}{3}$

13. $1\frac{3}{8} \div 1\frac{1}{7}$

Multiply. Simplify if possible.

14. $5\frac{1}{4} \times 4\frac{2}{3}$

15. $3\frac{3}{5} \times 2\frac{6}{7}$

SOLVE on Your Own

Skills Practice

Convert the improper fraction.

When converting mixed numbers into improper fractions, remember to add the original numerator to the product of the whole number and the denominator.

1. $2\frac{1}{4}$ _____

2. $3\frac{3}{7}$ _____

3. $5\frac{1}{2}$ _____

4. $2\frac{6}{7}$ _____

5. $7\frac{2}{3}$ _____

Multiply. Simplify if possible.

6. $\frac{2}{5} \times 1\frac{4}{5}$ _____

7. $3\frac{3}{7} \times \frac{7}{4}$ _____

8. $4\frac{1}{2} \times 3\frac{1}{9}$ _____

9. $2\frac{3}{5} \times 2\frac{2}{3}$ _____

10. $1\frac{2}{5} \times 5\frac{1}{2}$ _____

Divide. Simplify if possible.

11. $3\frac{3}{4} \div 2\frac{3}{4}$ _____

12. $1\frac{2}{5} \div 1\frac{3}{4}$ _____

13. $\frac{3}{4} \div 6\frac{1}{2}$ _____

14. $1\frac{4}{5} \div 2\frac{3}{8}$ _____

15. $3\frac{6}{7} \div 3\frac{1}{2}$ _____

Multiplying and Dividing Mixed Numbers

Strategies

Find a Pattern, Try a Simpler Form of the Problem

Step 1: Read On his first attempt, James threw a shot put $6\frac{2}{3}$ feet. After a week of practice, he threw the shot put five times farther. How far did James throw the shot put after a week of practice?

STRATEGY	SOLUTION
Find a Pattern When you have a mixed number multiple, you can make a list of multiples in order to find a pattern to help you find the actual answer.	**Step 2: Plan** List the distances that are one, two, and three times the first amount. Then look for a pattern. If there is an obvious pattern, extend it to include five times the first amount. **Step 3: Solve** James threw the shot put $6\frac{2}{3}$ feet to start. First, convert this to an improper fraction: $6\frac{2}{3} = \frac{20}{3}$ Next, make a list of this distance times 0, 1, 2, and 3: $0, \frac{20}{3}, \frac{40}{3}, \frac{60}{3}$ This appears to show a pattern. The numerator increases by 20 as the shot put is thrown x times farther. To solve the problem, extend the pattern. $0, \frac{20}{3}, \frac{40}{3}, \frac{60}{3}, \frac{80}{3}, \frac{100}{3}$ So, $5 \times 6\frac{2}{3} = \frac{100}{3} = 33\frac{1}{3}$ ft. **Step 4: Check** Multiply mixed numbers to find the answer. To multiply mixed numbers, first convert them to improper fractions. Then multiply the numerators, multiply the denominators, and simplify the fraction if possible. $5 \times 6\frac{2}{3} = \frac{5}{1} \times \frac{20}{3} = \frac{100}{3} = 33\frac{1}{3}$ ft. The answer checks.
Try a Simpler Form of the Problem Mixed numbers can be rewritten as the sum of the whole part and the fractional part. For example, $3\frac{1}{2} = 3 + \frac{1}{2}$. When a problem requires multiplying with a mixed number, it is sometimes simpler to rewrite the mixed number as an addition expression and then use the distributive property.	**Step 2: Plan** Find $5 \times 6\frac{2}{3}$ ft by using the distributive property to rewrite the problem as the sum of two simpler multiplication problems. **Step 3: Solve** $5 \times 6\frac{2}{3} = 5 \times (6 + \frac{2}{3}) = (5 \times 6) + (5 \times \frac{2}{3}) =$ $30 + \frac{10}{3} = 30 + 3\frac{1}{3} = 33\frac{1}{3}$ So, $5 \times 6\frac{2}{3}$ ft $= 33\frac{1}{3}$ ft. **Step 4: Check** Rewrite $6\frac{2}{3}$ as an improper fraction, multiply, and write the answer as a mixed number: $5 \times 6\frac{2}{3} = \frac{5}{1} \times \frac{20}{3} = \frac{100}{3} = 33\frac{1}{3}$.

YOUR TURN

Choose the Right Word

> distributive property
> mixed number   reciprocal

Fill in each blank with the correct word or phrase from the box.

1. You could rewrite $2 \times (3 + 5)$ as $(2 \times 3) +$ (2×5) using the _____.

2. The _____ of a fraction is the fraction "flipped over," with the numerator and denominator switched.

3. A _____ has a whole number part and a fraction part.

Yes or No?

Answer these questions and be ready to explain your answers.

4. Can $5 \times (6 + 3)$ be rewritten as $(5 + 6) \times (5 + 3)$? _____

5. Should you convert improper fractions to mixed numbers before multiplying? _____

6. Is a mixed number equal to the sum of its whole part and fractional part? _____

7. Is an improper fraction always less than or equal to one? _____

8. Is a mixed number always greater than one? _____

Show That You Know

Multiply or divide the mixed numbers.

Put your answers in simplest form.

9. $2\frac{1}{4} \times 3\frac{2}{3}$

10. $7\frac{1}{8} \times 1\frac{1}{6}$

11. $3\frac{2}{3} \div 4\frac{1}{2}$

12. $12\frac{2}{5} \div 3\frac{1}{10}$

Solve these word problems by multiplying or dividing mixed numbers. Put your answers in simplest form.

13. Maria ran $2\frac{1}{4}$ miles yesterday. Today she ran $1\frac{1}{3}$ times as far. How far did Maria run today?

14. Javier set a new high-jump record by jumping $3\frac{5}{8}$ ft. This was $1\frac{1}{4}$ times higher than the old record. What was the old record?

READ on Your Own

Reading Comprehension Strategy: Previewing/Predicting

Intense Sports, *pages 13–14*

Before You Read

Think about the games you read about in "Curling, Bowling, and Bocce." Which of the three games do you think you would like best?

As You Read

Preview "On Track," pages 13–15.

Write down what you know after previewing these pages. Make two predictions about things the article will tell you.

Read "On Track," pages 13–15.

Then fill in the chart below.

On Track	
What I know: _____ _____	Did your predictions match what you read about or did you have to make revisions? Explain. _____ _____
My predictions: (1) _____ _____ (2) _____ _____	_____ _____ _____ _____

After You Read

What track-and-field events do you think you would like to participate in? Why?

_____

_____

VOCABULARY

Watch for the words you are learning about.

decathlon: a men's athletic event made up of ten track-and-field events: three races, high jump, long jump, shot put, discus throw, javelin throw, hurdles, and pole vault

discus: a heavy disk that is thrown for distance in a track-and-field event

endurance: the ability keep doing an activity that is difficult to do for a long time

heptathlon: a women's athletic event made up of seven track-and-field events: two races, high jump, long jump, shot put, javelin throw, and hurdles

javelin: a thin, slender, and usually metal pole that is thrown for distance in a track-and-field event

Fluency Tip

Preview the text to make sure you can pronounce all names and difficult words.

SOLVE on Your Own

Intense Sports, *page 15*

Organize the Information

Read You Do the Math on magazine page 15. Then fill in the following flowchart to help you remember how to multiply or divide mixed numbers.

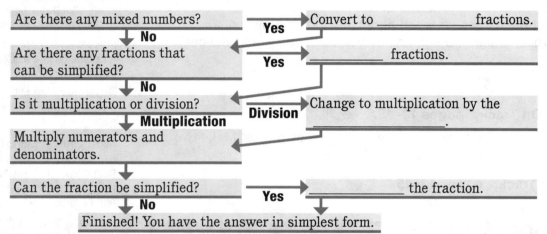

Are there any mixed numbers? _____ **Yes** ➔ Convert to _____ fractions.

↓ **No**

Are there any fractions that can be simplified? _____ **Yes** ➔ _____ fractions.

↓ **No**

Is it multiplication or division? _____ **Division** ➔ Change to multiplication by the _____.

↓ **Multiplication**

Multiply numerators and denominators. _____

↓

Can the fraction be simplified? _____ **Yes** ➔ _____ the fraction.

↓ **No**

Finished! You have the answer in simplest form.

You Do the Math

Use the flowchart above to help answer these questions. Write your answers in the space provided.

> **Using a flowchart will help you remember the steps to multiply or divide mixed numbers.**

1. Decide how many people should be on Rocco's team and then find the total number of hours the team members practice each day. What should you do if your answer is a mixed number?

   _____

   _____

2. What should you do next to find how many days Rocco's team should practice to reach 100 hours? Explain each step.

   _____

   _____

After You Solve

How else could you represent the information in the flowchart? Explain your answer.

_____

 **Solve It!**

The Four-Step Problem-Solving Plan

Step 1: Read	Step 2: Plan	Step 3: Solve	Step 4: Check
Make sure you understand what the problem is asking.	Decide how you will solve the problem.	Solve the problem using your plan.	Check to make sure your answer is correct.

Read the article below. Then answer the questions.

Open-Water Swimming

There are many water sports. Some are team events, such as crew or water polo. Others are individual sports, or sports that one person does. One individual event is open-water swimming.

Open-water swimming is any swimming done in large bodies of water such as lakes, bays, or oceans. However, it also means long-distance swimming for fitness or a contest. It can be part of a larger event, such as the first stage of a triathlon. It may be its own event, such as the 10 kilometer open-water swimming event that is now part of the Summer Olympics.

One popular goal among open-water swimmers is to swim the English Channel. This is a distance of 34 kilometers. There have been so many attempts that there are two groups, which set rules for the crossings. In order to have your crossing of the channel recognized, you must accept and obey these rules.

1. To convert kilometers to miles, divide the distance in kilometers by $1\frac{3}{5}$. What is the distance across the English Channel in miles?

   _____

   _____

2. Can open–water swimming be done in a pool? Explain why or why not.

   _____

   _____

   _____

   _____

YOUR TURN

Read the article below. Then answer the questions.

Windsurfing

Windsurfing is a sport that joins sail boating, snowboarding, skateboarding, and skiing. It is possible to learn the basic elements of windsurfing in only a few hours by taking a class, but mastering the board takes a lot of practice.

Do not be fooled by the size of the windsurfer's board. Although it is small—and may even look like it could be easily damaged—a windsurfer holds the World Speed Sailing Record at $48\frac{7}{10}$ knots (or about 56 mph). New global positioning system (GPS) equipment makes it possible for the windsurfing community to hold unplanned contests. Although these contests are not recognized by any special organization, or group, they encourage the enthusiast, or someone excited about the sport, to go even faster.

Fluency Tip

Emphasize important phrases, making sure to read them clearly.

1. How does the above photograph help you understand the article?

   _____

   _____

   _____

2. According to the article, how has GPS technology affected windsurfers?

   _____

   _____

3. Suppose your personal windsurfing speed record was $\frac{1}{4}$ of the world record. What would your record be in knots?

   _____

   _____

READ on Your Own

Reading Comprehension Strategy: Previewing/Predicting

Intense Sports, *pages 16–18*

Before You Read

Consider the decathlon events you read about in "On Track." The decathlon tests speed, strength, and endurance. What do you think the sport of cave diving would test in a person?

As You Read

Preview "Cave Diving," pages 16–18.

Write your prediction by completing the first sentence below.

Read "Cave Diving," pages 16–18.

Complete the remaining sentences.

I predict "Cave Diving" will be about

_____

_____

I correctly predicted that

_____

What I didn't know was that

_____

_____

After You Read

In what ways is cave diving an intense sport? Explain your answer.

_____

_____

_____

VOCABULARY

Watch for the words you are learning about.

nitrogen narcosis: an effect of deep water diving that leads to loss of muscle control and unclear thinking

Fluency Tip

Pay attention to punctuation and pause between phrases and sentences.

SOLVE on Your Own

Intense Sports, *page 19*

Organize the Information

Complete the flowchart using the information you find in the Math Project on magazine page 19.

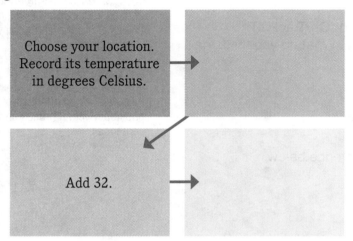

Choose your location. Record its temperature in degrees Celsius.

Add 32.

Drawing a picture or using a model can also help you solve this problem.

Math Project

Use the information in the flowchart above to answer these questions. Write your answers in the space provided.

1. Which location did you choose for your cave dive?

   _____

2. What expression did you write to calculate the temperature in degrees Fahrenheit?

   _____

After You Solve

How could you express the same information in the flowchart by drawing a picture or using a model?

_____

_____

Put It Together

Dividing Fractions

You have learned that the most common method for dividing fractions is to multiply by the reciprocal. Example: $3 \div \frac{1}{2} = 3 \times \frac{2}{1} = 6$. You should understand why this method works. There are several ways to model this example to explain why multiplying by the reciprocal gives the correct answer. One way to model this problem uses three rectangles.

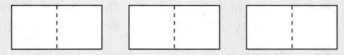

Remember that one way to think about a division problem is to ask "How many times does the divisor go into the dividend?" For example, if the problem is $8 \div 4$, think "How many fours go into eight?" Likewise, for the problem $3 \div \frac{1}{2}$, we can ask "How many halves are there in three?" We can draw a model of three rectangles divided into halves to help us visualize the problem.

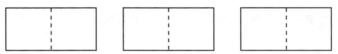

As you can see, there are two halves in each of the three rectangles, or $3 \times 2 = 6$ total halves in three. So, $3 \div \frac{1}{2} = 3 \times 2 = 6$.

Notice that we multiplied the dividend (3) by 2 to find $3 \div \frac{1}{2}$. This is because $\frac{2}{1}$ is the reciprocal of $\frac{1}{2}$.

Practicing Dividing Fractions

For each problem, draw a model like the one in the above example. Use your model to find the answer.

1. $2 \div \frac{1}{3} = $ _____

2. $4 \div \frac{1}{5} = $ _____

3. $1\frac{1}{2} \div \frac{1}{2} = $ _____

4. $2\frac{3}{5} \div \frac{1}{5} = $ _____

YOUR TURN

Thinking About Dividing Fractions

Did you know that division problems can be written as fractions? Learning to think of division problems as fractions can help you practice both division and simplifying fractions. If you can quickly recall certain division facts, you can use those facts to find the simplest form of those fractions. Look at the example below:

> Seth, Kyoto, and Derrick bought a pack of 15 game cards. They want to share the cards equally between the three of them. How can they use fractions to help divide the cards?
>
> 15 cards ÷ 3 friends can be rewritten as $\frac{15}{3}$.
>
> Each friend gets $\frac{15}{3}$, or fifteen-thirds, of the cards. This amounts to five cards each.
>
> Changing division problems into fractions works because another way to think about fractions is the numerator divided by the denominator.
>
> Rewriting division problems as fractions can help you understand the quotient when it is not a whole number.
>
> For example: $8 \div 3 = \frac{8}{3} = 2\frac{2}{3}$.
>
> It is easier to think of the quotient as the familiar fraction $2\frac{2}{3}$, rather than as a decimal or as a remainder.

Rewrite the following division problems as fractions. Then use the fractions to find the quotient.

Write the quotient as a mixed number if needed.

1. 9 ÷ 1 _____

2. 20 ÷ 4 _____

3. 13 ÷ 2 _____

4. 85 ÷ 9 _____

5. 8 ÷ 24 _____

6. 15 ÷ 100 _____

Show That You Know

Read the information below. Use what you read about dividing fractions to answer the questions. Use the space provided to show your work.

Anthony runs an online site that sells a variety of balls used in different sports. To figure out how much to charge customers for shipping, he makes a table to show the weight for some of the balls in pounds:

Type of Ball	Weight (lb.)
Baseball	$\frac{1}{3}$
Basketball	$1\frac{1}{3}$
Bowling Ball	10
Tennis Ball	$\frac{1}{8}$

1. Suppose Anthony can pack 3 pounds of tennis balls into a small box. How many tennis balls are there in 3 pounds? Draw a model to show the problem and solve.

2. How many times heavier is the basketball than the baseball? Draw a model to show the problem and solve.

3. How many times heavier are the bowling balls Anthony sells than a baseball? Write a division expression and solve to answer the question.

Show That You Know (continued)

4. Not including the box or packing materials, a box of bowling balls weighs 20 pounds. How many bowling balls are in the box? Write a division expression to show the problem and then rewrite it as a fraction and simplify to solve.

5. A different website sells a 12 pound bowling ball. How many times heavier is a 12 pound ball than the 10 pound ball? Write the problem as a fraction and then simplify to solve.

6. Suppose Anthony charges $8 to ship 12 baseballs. How much does he charge for each pound?

Review What You've Learned

7. What have you learned in this Connections lesson about dividing fractions?

_____

_____

8. What have you learned in this Connections lesson that you did not already know?

_____

_____

9. What have you learned in this lesson about the relationship between division and fractions that will help you solve other problems?

_____

_____

_____

Review and Practice

Skills Review

Multiplying fractions:

To multiply fractions, multiply the numerators and then multiply the denominators.

$$\frac{3}{22} \times \frac{4}{10} = \frac{(3 \times 4)}{(22 \times 10)} = \frac{12}{220}$$

$\frac{12}{220}$ can be simplified to $\frac{3}{55}$.

The fractions may be simplified before multiplying.

Finding a fraction of a number:

You can use multiplication to find a fraction of a number. For example, to find $\frac{2}{3}$ of five, multiply five by $\frac{2}{3}$:

$$5 \times \frac{2}{3} = \frac{5}{1} \times \frac{2}{3} = \frac{10}{3} = 3\frac{1}{3}. \text{ So, } 3\frac{1}{3} \text{ is } \frac{2}{3} \text{ of five.}$$

Reciprocal:

The reciprocal of a number is the number that it must be multiplied by to get a product of one.

$\frac{4}{7}$ inverted is $\frac{7}{4}$. $\frac{7}{4}$ is the reciprocal of $\frac{4}{7}$.

$$\frac{4}{7} \times \frac{7}{4} = \frac{28}{28} = 1$$

Dividing fractions:

To divide fractions, multiply the first fraction (the dividend) by the reciprocal of the second fraction (the divisor).

$$\frac{1}{3} \div \frac{2}{5} = \frac{1}{3} \times \frac{5}{2} = \frac{5}{6}$$

Multiplying mixed numbers:

When multiplying mixed numbers, first change them into improper fractions. Multiply the fractions and simplify the product.

$$1\frac{3}{7} \times 2\frac{4}{5} =$$

$$\frac{10}{7} \times \frac{14}{5} = \frac{140}{35} = 4$$

Dividing mixed numbers:

When dividing with mixed numbers, first change them into improper fractions. Then divide the fractions as you normally would.

$$1\frac{2}{5} \div 4\frac{1}{3} = \frac{7}{5} \div \frac{13}{3}$$

$$\frac{7}{5} \div \frac{13}{3} = \frac{7}{5} \times \frac{3}{13} = \frac{21}{65}$$

Strategy Review

- If you are confused by a word problem with difficult fractions, change the complicated fractions to fractions that are easier to work with as you figure out what to do. Once you have a plan to solve the problem, solve it with the original fractions.

- You can use a model to help multiply fractions. Divide a rectangle into rows and use one color to show the first fraction. Then divide the rectangle into columns and use a second color to show the second fraction. The overlapping colors show the product.

- When multiplying a mixed number, you can rewrite the mixed number as an addition expression and then use the distributive property to find the product.

Skills and Strategies Practice

Write your answer to each exercise in the space provided.

1. Multiply $\frac{1}{4} \times \frac{1}{8}$.

_____

2. Divide $\frac{13}{9} \div \frac{4}{9}$.

_____

3. Divide $\frac{3}{8} \div \frac{2}{7}$.

_____

4. Multiply $8\frac{2}{3} \times \frac{1}{3}$.

_____

5. Divide $\frac{5}{8} \div \frac{3}{7}$.

_____

Be sure you understand what a test question is asking. Read it twice if necessary. Do this to avoid confusion between multiplication and division. $\frac{3}{12} \times \frac{2}{7}$ is not the same as $\frac{3}{12} \div \frac{2}{7}$. These are different problems with different answers. You want to be sure you are answering the correct problem.

Mid-Unit Review

Circle the letter of the correct answer.

1. $\frac{1}{3} \times \frac{2}{7} = $ _____

   A. $\frac{2}{7}$ C. $\frac{2}{21}$

   B. $\frac{1}{21}$ D. $\frac{7}{6}$

2. $\frac{1}{8} \div \frac{2}{3} = $ _____

   A. $\frac{1}{12}$ C. $\frac{16}{3}$

   B. $\frac{3}{16}$ D. $\frac{3}{8}$

3. $\frac{8}{9} \times \frac{7}{11} = $ _____

   A. $\frac{88}{63}$ C. $\frac{56}{99}$

   B. $\frac{56}{20}$ D. $\frac{64}{99}$

4. $5\frac{7}{9} \times 13\frac{2}{3}$ is the same as _____.

   A. $\frac{52}{9} \times \frac{3}{41}$ C. $\frac{51}{9} \times \frac{40}{3}$

   B. $\frac{52}{9} \times \frac{41}{3}$ D. $\frac{53}{9} \times \frac{41}{3}$

5. What is the reciprocal of $\frac{3}{49}$?

   A. 49   C. $\frac{49}{3}$

   B. 3   D. 1

6. $\frac{1}{5} \times \frac{3}{10} = $ _____

   A. $\frac{12}{100}$ C. $\frac{8}{3}$

   B. $\frac{7}{200}$ D. $\frac{3}{50}$

7. $\frac{1}{12} \div \frac{12}{7} = $ _____

   A. $\frac{7}{108}$ C. $\frac{7}{12}$

   B. 1   D. $\frac{7}{144}$

8. $3 \times 7\frac{1}{3} = $ _____

   A. 21   C. 23

   B. 22   D. 24

9. $\frac{13}{9} \times 4 = $ _____

   A. $\frac{1}{3}$ C. $\frac{25}{12}$

   B. $\frac{27}{157}$ D. $\frac{52}{9}$

10. $1\frac{4}{5} \times \frac{3}{2} = $ _____

    A. $\frac{27}{5}$ C. 3

    B. $2\frac{7}{10}$ D. $2\frac{4}{5}$

11. $\frac{3}{7} \div \frac{1}{9} = $ _____

    A. $\frac{4}{63}$ C. $\frac{27}{7}$

    B. $\frac{1}{21}$ D. $\frac{27}{9}$

12. $\frac{22}{3} \times \frac{1}{7} = $ _____

    A. $1\frac{1}{21}$ C. $9\frac{3}{7}$

    B. $1\frac{2}{21}$ D. $\frac{21}{22}$

Mid-Unit Review

13. $6\frac{2}{3} \div 2\frac{3}{5} =$ _____

   A. $\frac{95}{39}$ C. $\frac{95}{36}$

   B. $\frac{100}{36}$ D. $\frac{100}{39}$

14. $\frac{40}{11} \div \frac{3}{5} =$ _____

   A. $\frac{120}{55}$ C. $\frac{200}{11}$

   B. $\frac{43}{16}$ D. $\frac{200}{33}$

15. $\frac{8}{4} \times \frac{4}{2} =$ _____

   A. 5   C. 4

   B. $\frac{31}{8}$ D. $\frac{12}{8}$

16. $1\frac{4}{10} \div 1\frac{2}{5} =$ _____

   A. 1   C. $1\frac{1}{5}$

   B. $1\frac{1}{2}$ D. 2

17. $\frac{3}{4} \div \frac{10}{9} =$ _____

   A. $\frac{10}{12}$ C. $\frac{5}{6}$

   B. $\frac{27}{40}$ D. $\frac{29}{40}$

18. $\frac{8}{3} \times \frac{3}{13} =$ _____

   A. $\frac{27}{39}$ C. $\frac{8}{13}$

   B. $\frac{22}{39}$ D. $\frac{11}{13}$

19. $2\frac{2}{7} \div 1\frac{1}{9} =$ _____

   A. $\frac{99}{70}$ C. $\frac{70}{99}$

   B. $\frac{160}{63}$ D. $\frac{144}{70}$

20. $\frac{1}{2} \div \frac{14}{9} =$ _____

   A. $\frac{7}{9}$ C. $\frac{9}{7}$

   B. $\frac{9}{28}$ D. $3\frac{1}{3}$

21. $4\frac{2}{3} \times 3\frac{5}{9} =$ _____

   A. $\frac{448}{27}$ C. $\frac{12}{27}$

   B. $\frac{378}{15}$ D. $\frac{270}{36}$

22. $\frac{3}{4} \times \frac{5}{12} =$ _____

   A. $\frac{8}{48}$ C. $\frac{15}{48}$

   B. $\frac{1}{2}$ D. $\frac{1}{6}$

23. $\frac{3}{20} \div \frac{3}{20} =$ _____

   A. 1   C. $\frac{6}{20}$

   B. $\frac{9}{20}$ D. $\frac{6}{40}$

24. $1\frac{1}{10} \times 1\frac{1}{10} =$ _____

   A. $\frac{121}{10}$ C. $\frac{121}{1}$

   B. $\frac{121}{100}$ D. $\frac{11}{10}$

Expressing Decimals in Scientific Notation

Learn the SKILL

Gina's science class is learning about bacteria. According to her textbook, the length of an E. coli bacterium, in scientific notation, is only 8×10^{-5} inches. How can Gina rewrite the length as a decimal?

SKILL	EXAMPLE	COMPLETE THE EXAMPLE
When an exponent is a negative **integer**, multiply the reciprocal of the base by itself the number of times shown by the exponent.	The reciprocal of 10 is $\frac{1}{10}$, so $10^{-5} =$ $\frac{1}{10} \times \frac{1}{10} \times \frac{1}{10} \times \frac{1}{10} \times \frac{1}{10} =$ $\frac{1}{100,000}$. $8 \times 10^{-5} = \frac{8}{1} \times \frac{1}{100,000} =$ $\frac{8}{100,000} = 0.00008$	Write 9×10^{-3} as a decimal. _____
An easy way to rewrite something in **scientific notation** is to simply move the decimal point on the first number. If the exponent is negative, move the decimal point to the left the number of places shown by the exponent.	To write 8×10^{-5} as a decimal move the decimal point in the first number to the left five times: 8. Then fill in the spaces with zeros. .00008 = 0.00008	Write 2.1×10^{-5}. _____
To write a decimal in scientific notation, simply reverse the above process. Remember to move the decimal point to the right, not the left.	To write 0.0032 in scientific notation, move the decimal point to the right until the three is in the ones place: 0.0032 The decimal point had to be moved three places, so $0.0032 = 3.2 \times 10^{-3}$.	Write 0.000091 in scientific notation. _____

YOUR TURN

Choose the Right Word

> base   exponent   integer
> scientific notation

Fill in each blank with the correct word or phrase from the box.

1. _____ is a way to write very large or very small numbers as a number multiplied by 10 raised to an integer exponent.

2. In the expression 3^2, the number three is the _____ and the number two is the _____.

3. A(n) _____ can be a whole number or a corresponding negative number.

Yes or No?

Answer these questions and be ready to explain your answers.

4. Can two hundredths be written in scientific notation? _____

5. Does a negative exponent mean the number is negative? _____

6. Can the number 46 be written with a negative exponent? _____

7. To rewrite 2.5×10^{-2}, do you move the decimal point in 2.5 to the right two places? _____

8. Is −2.5 an integer? _____

Show That You Know

Write as a decimal number.

9. $10^{-1} =$

10. $10^{-3} =$

11. $10^{-5} =$

Write in scientific notation.

12. $0.03 =$

13. $0.01 =$

14. $0.5 =$

15. $0.0001 =$

SOLVE on Your Own

Skills Practice

When you change scientific notation to standard form, move the decimal point to the left when the exponent is negative.

Write the number as a decimal.

1. 2×10^{-3} _____

2. 3×10^{-1} _____

3. 10^{-6} _____

4. 2×10^{-4} _____

5. 1.2×10^{-2} _____

6. 10^{-1} _____

7. 4.2×10^{-1} _____

8. 7.9×10^{-5} _____

Write the number in scientific notation.

9. 0.002 _____

10. 0.014 _____

11. 0.00003 _____

12. 0.00035 _____

13. 0.0000001 _____

14. 0.0589 _____

15. 0.1657 _____

16. 0.0000047 _____

Expressing Decimals in Scientific Notation

Strategies

Find a Pattern, Try a Simpler Form of the Problem

Step 1: Read A modem sends information to the internet as "ones" and "zeros." The less time it takes the modem to send a one or a zero, the faster the internet connection. Suppose it takes Marvin's cable modem 5.8×10^{-6} of a second to send a single one or a zero. How can he write this time as a decimal?

STRATEGY	SOLUTION
Find a Pattern Finding a pattern between the exponent in scientific notation and the number of zeros in decimal form can help you convert numbers from one form to the other.	**Step 2: Plan** Write 5.8×10^{-6} as a decimal by converting simpler numbers first and then continuing the pattern. **Step 3: Solve** $5.8 \times 10^{-1} = 0.58$ $5.8 \times 10^{-2} = 0.058$ $5.8 \times 10^{-3} = 0.0058$ Notice the pattern: the number of zeros after the decimal point is one less than the exponent. $6 - 1 = 5$, so $5.8 \times 10^{-6} = 0.0000058$. **Step 4: Check** Write 0.0000058 in scientific notation. The decimal point must be moved six places to the right to put the five in the ones place, so $0.0000058 = 5.8 \times 10^{-6}$.
Try a Simpler Form of the Problem If the first factor of a number in scientific notation is not a whole number, try solving the problem without the numbers to the right of the decimal point. Remember to adjust your answer when you finish.	**Step 2: Plan** Rewrite 5×10^{-6} as a decimal. Then adjust the answer to find 5.8×10^{-6} in decimal form. **Step 3: Solve** $10^{-6} = \frac{1}{10} \times \frac{1}{10} \times \frac{1}{10} \times \frac{1}{10} \times \frac{1}{10} \times \frac{1}{10} = \frac{1}{1,000,000}$ $5 \times \frac{1}{1,000,000} = \frac{(5 \times 1)}{(1 \times 1,000,000)} =$ $\frac{5}{1,000,000} = 0.000005$ Add an eight to the right of the five to adjust the answer: $5.8 \times 10^{-6} = .0000058$ **Step 4: Check** Count the number of places the decimal point was moved to the left.

Choose the Right Word

> decimal   decimal point
> scientific notation   whole number

Fill each blank with the correct word or phrase from the box.

1. A _____ is a symbol that marks the beginning of the decimal place values.

2. 1.2×10^{-3} is an example of a number written in _____.

3. A _____ is a number such as 0, 1, 2, 3, 4, and so on.

4. A number with digits to the right of the ones place is a _____.

Yes or No?

Answer these questions and be ready to explain your answers.

5. Can any decimal number be expressed in scientific notation? _____

6. Is 2×10^5 equal to 2×10^{-5}? _____

7. If 1.7×10^{-5} is rewritten as a decimal, will there be four zeros to the right of the decimal point? _____

8. If 1.5×10^{-2} is rewritten as a decimal, will the five be in the thousandths place? _____

Show That You Know

Write each number in scientific notation.

9. 0.0258

10. 0.9762

11. 0.00371

12. 0.000000008313

Write each number in standard form.

13. 1.0175×10^{-2}

14. 8.2×10^{-7}

15. 2.36×10^{-5}

Use scientific notation to solve the following problem.

16. Using a microscope, a scientist measured various cells to be the following lengths.

Cell A: 10.6×10^{-5} cm; Cell B: 2.3×10^{-4} cm; Cell C: 0.0015 cm; Cell D: 107×10^{-6} cm.

Write the cells, in order of length, from longest to shortest. (Hint: Start by rewriting the numbers as decimals.)

READ on Your Own

Reading Comprehension Strategy: Previewing/Predicting

Intense Sports, *pages 20–21*

Fluency Tip

Try to read smoothly and expressively, just as a storyteller or news reporter would.

Before You Read

Think about what you read in "Cave Diving." Would you call cave diving an individual sport or a team sport? Why?

As You Read

Preview by reading the first paragraph of "Paintball: A Strategy Sport," pages 20–21.

In the chart below, write a prediction of what you think the reading will be about. Be sure to provide details about your prediction with some details.

Read "Paintball: A Strategy Sport," pages 20–21. (STOP)

If necessary, revise your prediction as you read. Then answer the question in the right column of the chart.

Paintball: A Strategy Sport	
Prediction: _____ _____ _____	Did your prediction match what you read about or did you have to revise your prediction as you read? Explain. _____ _____

After You Read

Have you ever played paintball or a similar sport, such as laser tag? If not, would you like to? Explain.

_____

_____

SOLVE on Your Own

Intense Sports, *page 22*

Organize the Information

Read You Do the Math on magazine page 22. Then fill out the following table with information on the winning averages for Stephan and his brother.

Player	Wins	Games Played	Average as Fraction	Average as Decimal
Stephan		60		
Patrick	95	250		
		185		

You Do the Math

Use the information in the table above to answer these questions. Write your answers in the space provided.

Gathering data in a table may help you find the answers to the magazine questions.

1. How did you find Patrick's average as a fraction and as a decimal?

_____

_____

2. How did you determine how many wins Stephan needed to have a better average?

_____

_____

_____

_____

After You Solve

What games do you play that you keep track of how many wins and losses you have? What is your winning average as a fraction and as a decimal?

_____

_____

Multiplying Decimals

Learn the SKILL

Savannah is mixing up a solution in her chemistry class. She is supposed to add 2.9 grams of salt for every liter of solution. If she needs to make 1.38 liters of solution, how much salt should she add?

SKILL	EXAMPLE	COMPLETE THE EXAMPLE
We learned earlier to multiply multidigit numbers. To do so, we have to multiply the first number by each digit of the second and add the partial products.	Multiply 21×13. $21 \times 3 = 63$ $21 \times 10 = 210$ $210 + 63 = 273$	Multiply 12×11. _____
To multiply decimals, add the partial products as you would if the decimal points were not there. Then count the total number of digits to the right of the decimal points in the factors and move the decimal point in the product so that an equal number of digits are to the right.	Multiply 1.38×2.9. $\quad\quad 1.38$ $\quad\underline{\times\ 2.9}$ $\quad\quad 1242$ $\quad\underline{+\ 2760}$ $\quad\quad 4002$ 1.38 has two digits to the right of the decimal point and 2.9 has one. $2 + 1 = 3$, so the decimal in the product belongs between the four and the zero: $1.38 \times 2.9 = 4.002$	Multiply 2.4×1.2. _____

Choose the Right Word

multiply   product   decimal   decimal point

Fill each blank with the correct word or phrase from the box.

1. The _____ is the dot in a decimal.

2. To _____ is to add a number to itself one or more times.

3. 0.785641 is an example of a number written in _____ form.

4. The _____ is the answer to a multiplication problem.

Yes or No?

Answer these questions and be ready to explain your answers.

5. Can two decimals be multiplied together? _____

6. When multiplying decimals, do you have to line the decimal points up? _____

7. Does the product of 3.6×2 have one digit after the decimal point? _____

8. Does the product of 3.67×1.2 have two digits after the decimal point? _____

Show That You Know

Multiply.

9. $6.7 \times 2 =$

10. $3.58 \times 9 =$

11. $11.1 \times 1 =$

12. $12.9 \times 13.1 =$

13. $11.57 \times 19.23 =$

14. $0.5 \times 0.5 =$

15. $0.3 \times 3 =$

SOLVE on Your Own

Skills Practice

Multiply.

When multiplying decimals, make sure you remember to place the decimal point in the product.

1. $0.21 \times 2 =$ _____

2. $0.99 \times 1.7 =$ _____

3. $0.01 \times 0.1 =$ _____

4. $11.9 \times 9.11 =$ _____

5. $0.4 \times 4 =$ _____

6. $0.4 \times 0.4 =$ _____

7. $0.04 \times 0.04 =$ _____

8. $0.002 \times 2 =$ _____

9. $0.014 \times 2.9 =$ _____

10. $0.00003 \times 2 =$ _____

11. $0.00035 \times 2.11 =$ _____

12. $0.0003 \times 12 =$ _____

13. $0.589 \times 2 =$ _____

14. $0.16 \times 1.34 =$ _____

Multiplying Decimals
Strategies
Draw a Picture or Use a Model, Make a List

Step 1: Read Shelly's store donates $0.10 of every dollar in sales to charity. If the store sells a picture frame for $6.00, how much will be donated to charity?

STRATEGY	SOLUTION
Draw a Picture or Use a Model A number line can help you multiply a decimal by a whole number. Use repeated addition or skip-counting to find the product of the two numbers on the number line.	Step 2: Plan Draw a number line and skip-count to find 0.10×6. Step 3: Solve Begin by drawing a number line. Label the line in tenths. 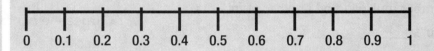 Begin at zero and then use skip-counting to add 0.10 six times. 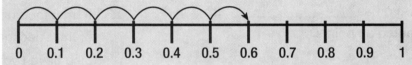 So $0.60 from the sale will be donated to charity. Step 4: Check Use repeated addition to check your answer: $0.10 \times 6 = 0.10 + 0.10 + 0.10 + 0.10 + 0.10 + 0.10 = 0.60$.
Make a List Sometimes making a list can help you use repeated addition to multiply a decimal by a whole number.	Step 2: Plan Make a list to organize using repeated addition to find 0.10×6. Step 3: Solve $$0.10 + 0.10 = 0.20$$ $$+ 0.10 = 0.30$$ $$+ 0.10 = 0.40$$ $$+ 0.10 = 0.50$$ $$+ 0.10 = 0.60$$ So $0.60 from the sale will be donated to charity. Step 4: Check Convert 0.10 to a fraction and use repeated addition to check: $0.10 = \frac{1}{10}$. $$\frac{1}{10} + \frac{1}{10} + \frac{1}{10} + \frac{1}{10} + \frac{1}{10} + \frac{1}{10} = \frac{6}{10}$$ Now convert $\frac{6}{10}$ to a decimal. $\frac{6}{10} = 0.60$. The answer is correct.

YOUR TURN

Choose the Right Word

> decimal   factor
> number line   whole number

Fill each blank with the correct word or phrase from the box.

1. The number 2.5 is not a
   _____, but the number 3 is.

2. A number multiplied by another number is
   called a _____.

3. A _____ has digits to the
   right of the decimal point.

4. Numbers on a _____ are
   represented as points.

Yes or No?

Answer these questions and be ready to explain your answers.

5. Can 1.3×0.4 be rewritten as
   $1.3 + 1.3 + 1.3 + 1.3$? _____

6. Can you use repeated addition to find
   the product of a decimal and a whole
   number? _____

7. Does the number of digits to the left of the
   decimal point in a product equal the total
   number of digits to the left of the decimal
   points in the factors? _____

8. If both factors have two digits to the right
   of their decimal points, will the product
   also have two digits to the right of its
   decimal point? _____

Show That You Know

Multiply the decimals.

9. 3.52×1.5

10. 11.07×2.01

11. 0.08×9.99

12. 654.02×0.0057

Solve each word problem by multiplying the decimals.

13. Allen has $428.60 in the bank. Carlos has 2.8 times
    that much money in his account. How much money
    does Carlos have in his account?

14. Ryan purchases a new helmet for $48.95. The sales
    tax rate is 0.065. How much sales tax does Ryan
    have to pay?

READ on Your Own

Reading Comprehension Strategy: Previewing/Predicting

Intense Sports, *pages 23–25*

VOCABULARY

Watch for the words you are learning about.

rapids: the part of a river where the current flows fast, usually over rocks

slalom: a timed race that takes place on a wavy course with upright poles that the athlete must zigzag between

Fluency Tip

As you read a new paragraph or page, vary your expression and volume.

Before You Read

Think about what you read in "Paintball: A Strategy Sport." What special equipment is needed for paintball?

As You Read

Preview "Whitewater Blast!" pages 23–25.
Write two predictions in the chart for these pages.

Read "Whitewater Blast!" pages 23–25. STOP
Complete the rest of the chart.

Prediction 1	Prediction 2
I predict	I predict
Information I predicted that was in the pages	Information I predicted that was in the pages
Information that was in the pages that I didn't predict	Information that was in the pages that I didn't predict

After You Read

Do you think you would prefer to paddle a kayak or a canoe? Why?

SOLVE on Your Own

Intense Sports, *page 25*

Organize the Information

Read You Do the Math on magazine page 25. Then complete the following table with information about the canoes passing through the rapids.

Number of Canoes	Length of Time to Pass the Rapids
1	
2	
3	
4	
5	
6	

Making a list of the times may help you answer the magazine questions.

You Do the Math

Use the information in the table above to answer these questions.
Write your answers in the space provided.

1. How did you fill in the column for the length of time to pass the rapids?

_____

_____

2. How would you find the time for 3.5 canoes to pass the rapids? What would that mean?

_____

_____

After You Solve

Besides canoes and kayaks, what other types of boats can you think of? Have you ever been on any of them?

_____

_____

Solve It!

The Four-Step Problem-Solving Plan

Step 1: Read	Step 2: Plan	Step 3: Solve	Step 4: Check
Make sure you understand what the problem is asking.	Decide how you will solve the problem.	Solve the problem using your plan.	Check to make sure your answer is correct.

Read the article below. Then answer the questions.

Baseball

Baseball is often referred to as the national pastime because it is so popular. Each summer, more than 70 million Americans go to ballparks to watch major-league baseball games being played.

Most games end after nine innings; the team with the most runs then wins the game. However, if the score is tied after nine innings, more innings are played. The most innings ever played in a single major-league game is 26. This 26-inning game was played in Boston in 1920.

Even when a game has only nine innings, the time it takes to play the game can vary a lot. Sometimes batters strike out quickly, and the game is over fast. Other times, play is paused when there is rain or bad weather. The playing starts again if the rain stops. Fans should expect to stay anywhere from two to five hours if they want to see all of a baseball game. That is part of what makes baseball interesting— every game is different!

1. How many Americans go to watch live major-league baseball games every year?

   _____

2. Suppose in one year, 39 million people went to see a baseball game. The following year, 1.6 times as many people went to a game. How many people saw a game that year?

   _____

3. A game played on Sunday took 10 innings. A game played on Wednesday had 1.3 times as many innings. How many innings were there in Wednesday's game?

   _____

YOUR TURN

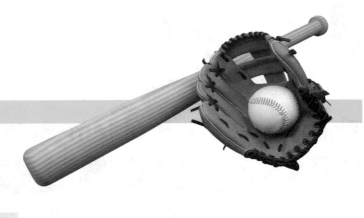

Read the article below. Then answer the questions.

Longest and Shortest Baseball Games

Just because a game has many innings does not mean that it will take an unusually long number of hours to play. In 1920, one baseball game had 26 innings, but lasted just under four hours. The major-league baseball game with the record for taking the longest time to play was played in 1984. In that game, the Milwaukee Brewers played the Chicago White Sox for just over eight hours. The game had 25 innings.

The shortest major-league baseball game that lasted a full nine innings was played in 1919. This game between New York and Philadelphia took place in New York and lasted just 51 minutes.

No matter how many innings are played or how many hours a baseball game lasts, passionate baseball fans are sure to enjoy themselves.

1. Suppose the first inning of a baseball game lasts for 12 minutes. If the second inning is 1.75 times as long as the first, for how many minutes does the second inning last?

_____

2. The teams from which two cities played the shortest major-league baseball game to last a full nine innings?

_____

_____

Fluency Tip

Take your time when reading complex material so you can make sense of difficult ideas.

READ on Your Own

Reading Comprehension Strategy: Previewing/Predicting

Intense Sports, *pages 26–28*

Fluency Tip

As you read and reread, choose a pace that lets you understand what you read.

Before You Read

Think about the sports you read about in "Whitewater Blast!" Why are canoeing and kayaking competitions intense?

As You Read

Checking your predictions as you read will help you know whether you understand the text.

First, preview "America's Favorite Sport," pages 26–28.

Then, predict what the passage will be about. Write your prediction below.

I predict "America's Favorite Sport" will be about

_____

_____

Now carefully read "America's Favorite Sport," pages 26–28.

Then, check whether your prediction matched the text.

Did your prediction match the text, or did you have to revise it? Explain.

_____

_____

After You Read

Do you enjoy baseball games? Would you rather play or watch the game? Explain your answer.

_____

_____

SOLVE on Your Own

Intense Sports, *page 29*

Organize the Information

Use a table to organize the information you find in the Math Project on magazine page 29. You can make a similar table for each player on the Little League team.

	Hits	Hits ÷ at Bats	Slugging Percentage of Each Type of Hit
Singles	5		1 × _____ = _____
Doubles	2		2 × _____ = _____
Triples	0		3 × _____ = _____
Home runs	1		4 × _____ = _____
Slugging percentage (add the products in column 4)			

Math Project

Use the information in the table above and in tables you create to answer these questions. Write your answers in the space provided.

1. How can you find the slugging percentage for a player using fractions instead of decimals?

   _____

   _____

2. Explain your thinking in how you chose the hitters in the third and fifth spots in the batting order.

   _____

   _____

   _____

After You Solve

How could you organize the table in a different way?

_____

_____

Dividing Decimals

Learn the SKILL

Edward and Maggie are going to play ping pong. The table is 108.9 inches long. Edward and Maggie are trying to find the middle of the table. They divide 108.9 by two to find where the net should go.

VOCABULARY

Watch for the words you are learning about.

long division: the process used to break multidigit numbers into a series of easier steps

SKILL	EXAMPLE	COMPLETE THE EXAMPLE
You learned earlier how to use **long division** to divide multidigit numbers. To do so, divide the divisor into each digit of the dividend from left to right.	Divide $422 \div 2$. $\begin{array}{r} 211 \\ 2\overline{)422} \end{array}$	Divide $412 \div 4$. _____
To divide a decimal by a whole number, repeat the same steps as above, but place a decimal point in the quotient directly above the one in the dividend. If needed, you can add additional zeros to the right of the dividend without changing the value of the number.	Divide $108.9 \div 2$. $\begin{array}{r} 54.45 \\ 2\overline{)108.9} \end{array}$	Divide $24.2 \div 2$. _____
If the divisor is also a decimal, then move the decimal point to the right to make it a whole number. Then move the decimal point in the dividend the same number of places to the right and divide as before.	Divide $108.9 \div 0.2$. $0.2\overline{)108.9}$ Move the decimal point in 0.2 over one place to the right. So $\begin{array}{r} 544.5 \\ 2\overline{)1089.} \end{array} = 544.5$	Divide $2.4 \div 0.2$. _____

Learn the Skill

YOUR TURN

Choose the Right Word

dividend   divisor   long division   quotient

Fill each blank with the correct word or phrase from the box.

1. The process of breaking multidigit numbers into a series of easier steps is called _____.

2. The _____ is the number to be divided.

3. The _____ is the number that you divide by.

4. The _____ is the answer to a division problem.

Yes or No?

Answer these questions and be ready to explain your answers.

5. Can two decimals be divided by each other? _____

6. If the divisor is a whole number, does the decimal point of the dividend move? _____

7. If the divisor is a decimal, does the decimal point of the dividend move? _____

8. Does the quotient of $4.8 \div 0.2$ need a decimal point? _____

Show That You Know

Divide.

9. $6.8 \div 2 =$

10. $3.6 \div 9 =$

11. $11.1 \div 1 =$

12. $12.6 \div 0.6 =$

13. $11.2211 \div 0.11 =$

14. $0.5 \div 0.5 =$

15. $0.3 \div 3 =$

SOLVE on Your Own

Skills Practice

Divide.

If you move the decimal point in the divisor, remember to move the decimal point in the dividend the same direction and the same number of places.

1. 0.22 ÷ 2 = _____

2. 0.93 ÷ 0.3 = _____

3. 10 ÷ 0.1 = _____

8. 200.4 ÷ 0.04 = _____

4. 11.33 ÷ 0.11 = _____

9. 2 ÷ 0.002 = _____

5. 0.4 ÷ 0.4 = _____

10. 0.014 ÷ 2 = _____

6. 12.4 ÷ 0.02 = _____

11. 124.12 ÷ 0.1 = _____

7. 100.5 ÷ 5 = _____

12. 0.00035 ÷ 0.5 = _____

Dividing Decimals

Strategy

Guess, Check, and Revise

Step 1: Read Mira's team received a prize of $112.50. There were three people on Mira's team, and they decided to divide the money evenly amongst the team members. How much did each person get?

STRATEGY	SOLUTION
Guess, Check, and Revise One way to solve problems which involve dividing decimals is to use the inverse relationship between multiplication and division and the Guess, Check, and Revise problem solving strategy. Guess the solution and then use multiplication to check and revise your guess until it is correct.	Step 2: Plan Guess how much each teammate gets if the $112.50 is divided by three. Then use multiplication to check and revise the answer. Step 3: Solve Begin by making an educated guess. For example, you might try $40. Multiply your guess by three to check if $112.50, divided three ways, is $40: $40 × 3 = $120. $120 is too high, so revise your guess to a lesser amount. $38 × 3 = $114 and $37 × 3 = $111, so the solution must be between $37 and $38.

Try $37.50:

$$\begin{array}{r} \$37.50 \\ \times \qquad 3 \\ \hline \$112.50 \end{array}$$

So, $112.50 ÷ 3 = $37.50; each person gets $37.50.

Step 4: Check Use repeated subtraction to check your answer:

$$\begin{array}{r} \$112.50 \\ -\ \$\ 37.50 \\ \hline \$\ 75.00 \\ -\ \$\ 37.50 \\ \hline \$\ 37.50 \\ -\ \$\ 37.50 \\ \hline \$\ 00.00 \end{array}$$

YOUR TURN

Choose the Right Word

dividend   divisor   inverse operations

Fill each blank with the correct word or phrase from the box.

1. Multiplication and division are _____ because they undo each other.

2. In the expression 8.42 ÷ 1.32, the number 1.32 is the _____.

3. In a division problem, the _____ is the number to be divided.

Yes or No?

Answer these questions and be ready to explain your answers.

4. If the divisor and the dividend are both decimals, can the quotient be a whole number? _____

5. Is the product of the divisor and the quotient equal to the dividend? _____

6. When using the Guess, Check, and Revise problem-solving strategy, should you simply pick any number for your first guess? _____

7. If the divisor is a whole number and the dividend is a decimal, can the quotient be a whole number? _____

Show That You Know

Divide.

8. $241.20 ÷ 9

9. $108.65 ÷ 5

10. 37.05 ÷ 3

11. 685.727 ÷ 7

Solve each word problem by dividing decimals.

12. The school party planning committee has a budget of $457.84 to spend on four parties. If they divided the money evenly among the four parties, how much would be spent for each party?

13. Andre has 252.75 feet of kite string. If he divides the string evenly between four kites, how long will the string be on each kite?

READ on Your Own

Reading Comprehension Strategy: Previewing/Predicting

Intense Sports, *pages 30–31*

Before You Read

Remember what you read about in "America's Favorite Sport." Do baseball players need to be strong? Why or why not?

As You Read

Checking your predictions as you read will help you know whether you understand the text. As you read, remember to ask, "Does my prediction go along with what I am reading about?"

Preview "Who is the Strongest of Them All?" pages 30–31.

Use what you know to predict what this reading will be about. Write your prediction in the chart below.

Read "Who is the Strongest of Them All?" pages 30–31.

Complete the chart.

Preview, Read, and Predict	Read and Check
I predict that the article will be about _____ _____ _____	Did your prediction match the text, or did you have to revise it? Explain. _____ _____

After You Read

Which weightlifting exercise do you think is most useful?

_____

_____

SOLVE on Your Own

Intense Sports, *page 32*

Organize the Information

Read You Do the Math on magazine page 32. Then complete the following table with possible amounts of weight that Micah lifted.

	Guess 1	Guess 2	Guess 3
Day 1	100 lb	105 lb	
Day 2	110 lb		
Day 3	120 lb		
Day 4	130 lb		
Day 5	140 lb		
Average			125.5 lb

Listing possible answers may help you answer the magazine questions.

You Do the Math

Use the information in the table above to answer these questions. Write your answers in the space provided.

1. How did you find the average for the Guess 1 column?

   _____

2. How did you make the second guess?

   _____

3. How can you figure out how much more you need to increase each weight in order to get the desired average of 125.5 lb?

   _____

   _____

After You Solve

What do you think a powerlifter's body would look like? Why?

   _____

Solve It!

The Four-Step Problem-Solving Plan

Step 1: Read	Step 2: Plan	Step 3: Solve	Step 4: Check
Make sure you understand what the problem is asking.	Decide how you will solve the problem.	Solve the problem using your plan.	Check to make sure your answer is correct.

Read the article below. Then answer the questions.

Exercise

Exercise helps to keep our bodies healthy and to make us feel happy. Many people are on sports teams, take hikes on weekends, or take dance classes. However, many other people exercise very little. To help such people get started with regular exercise, health experts from the government's Centers for Disease Control and Prevention have suggested that certain steps be taken.

One step that these experts suggest is that people make exercise something that they do every day. This might involve activities that are normally considered exercise, like going to the gym, playing a sport, or participating in a physical education class. However, we can all get exercise daily by performing everyday activities. We might get exercise by walking or bicycling to school or work. Doing chores at home such as pulling weeds out of the garden and mowing the lawn are also good exercise.

1. How can people make exercise part of their everyday lives?

   _____

   _____

   _____

2. Imagine that four students ran a relay race at school. The race was 3.35 miles long, and each student ran the same distance. How far did each run?

   _____

YOUR TURN

Read the article below. Then answer the questions.

Exercise Levels

The amount of exercise that a person needs depends on the person's age and the type of exercise, among other things. It is recommended, or suggested, that young people get one hour of moderate-intensity exercise, which means not too hard and not too easy exercise, every day. Moderate-intensity exercise includes biking, walking fast, playing in a pool, and playing basketball for fun. During this type of action, the body burns about five calories per minute. A calorie is a measure of the energy in food.

For adults, health experts recommend that they do moderate-intensity exercise for one-half hour, at least five days each week. Adults could also get vigorous-intensity, or strong action, exercise for at least 20 minutes, three days each week. During vigorous-intensity exercise, more than seven calories are used every minute. Vigorous-intensity exercise includes activities like swimming laps, running, and jumping rope.

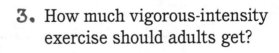

Fluency Tip

Use punctuation marks to help you read long sentences. Pause briefly for a comma and longer for a period.

1. What are three examples of moderate-intensity exercise?

   _____

   _____

2. Erika calculated that her body burned a total of 51 calories by exercising for 8.5 minutes. How many calories did she burn for each minute of exercise?

   _____

   _____

3. How much vigorous-intensity exercise should adults get?

   _____

4. Luke jogged 6.25 miles. If his body burned a total of 450.5 calories, how many calories did he burn for each mile he ran?

   _____

   _____

READ on Your Own

Reading Comprehension Strategy: Previewing/Predicting

Intense Sports, *pages 33–35*

Before You Read

Think about the lifting that you read about in "Who is the Strongest of Them All?" What type of exercise is powerlifting?

As You Read

Preview "Exercise—A Good Thing," pages 33–35.

Write a prediction of information you believe will be in the pages.

Information I predict will be in "Exercise—A Good Thing":

_____

_____

Read "Exercise—A Good Thing," pages 33–35.

Complete the question below.

Information that was in the pages that I did not expect:

_____

_____

After You Read

Do you do exercises every day that can improve your endurance or flexibility? If so, what are they?

_____

_____

VOCABULARY

Watch for the words you are learning about.

flexibility: capable of being bent; the ability to move easily through a full range of motion

Karvonen formula: a formula used to find a person's target heart rate

target heart rate: the goal number of heartbeats per minute during exercise that is good for the health of the heart

Fluency Tip

Preview the text to make sure you can pronounce all names and difficult words.

SOLVE on Your Own

Organize the Information

Use a table to organize the information you find in the Math Project on magazine page 36.

Activity	Number of Minutes Required to Burn 150 Calories	Number of Calories Burned in One Minute (150 Calories ÷ Column A)	Number of Minutes in the Week I Will Do the Exercise (Guess)	Number of Calories Burned
Jogging	15			
Biking quickly	13.3			
Walking quickly	29.5			
Playing volleyball	45			
Jumping rope	14.5			
			Total Calories Burned	

Math Project

Use the information in the table above to answer these questions. Write your answers in the space provided.

1. Which exercises do you want to do during the week? How many calories do these exercises burn in one minute?

2. Explain how you determined the number of minutes of each exercise you would do.

After You Solve

Is there other information that you could have listed in the table that would have made the problem easier to solve or a different way to organize the chart?

Put It Together · · · · · · · · · · · · · ·

Using Fractions to Understand Decimals

In the second half of this unit, you have learned the algorithms, or rules, for multiplying and dividing with decimals. Because fractions and decimals are related, we can use fractions to examine why these rules work.

When multiplying decimals, the total number of digits to the right of the decimal points in the factors determine where to place the decimal point in the product. For example:

$$0.2$$
$$\underline{\times\ 0.2}$$
$$0.04$$

Because $0.2 = \frac{2}{10}$, you could also write the problem as $\frac{2}{10} \times \frac{2}{10}$:

$$\frac{2}{10} \times \frac{2}{10} = \frac{(2 \times 2)}{(10 \times 10)} = \frac{4}{100} = .04$$

Notice that multiplying the numerators determines the digits in the final solution and then multiplying the denominators determines the location of the decimal point in the final solution. A tenth multiplied by a tenth equals a hundredth.

When the divisor in a division problem is a decimal, you can move the decimal point in the divisor and dividend to the right until the divisor becomes a whole number. For example:

$$1.6 \div 0.8 = 16 \div 8$$

But why doesn't this change the quotient?

Remember that a division expression can be rewritten as a fraction:

$$1.6 \div 0.8 = \frac{1.6}{0.8}$$

To find equivalent fractions, multiply the numerator and the denominator by the same factor:

$$\frac{(1.6 \times 10)}{(0.8 \times 10)} = \frac{16}{8}$$

So, $1.6 \div 0.8 = \frac{1.6}{0.8} = \frac{16}{8} = 16 \div 8$.

Practice Using Fractions to Understand Decimals

Rewrite each expression using fractions and solve. (Hint: Rewrite the division expression as a fraction.)

1. $0.2 \times 0.3 =$ _____

2. $0.1 \times 0.03 =$ _____

3. $0.8 \times 0.04 =$ _____

4. $0.056 \div 0.007 =$ _____

Thinking About Using Fractions to Understand Decimals

You have learned how multiplication and division of fractions can help you understand multiplication of decimals. Use what you've learned to answer the questions below.

1. What is the denominator of the product when tenths is multiplied by hundredths?

   _____

2. What simple rule can you use to determine the number of decimal places in a product?

   _____

3. What simple rule can you use to determine the number of decimal places in a quotient?

   _____

   _____

4. Think about where the decimal point would be placed in the product of 0.04 × 0.09.

   How many decimal places should there be in the product? _____

   What is the product? _____

   How would you rewrite the problem and answer as fractions? _____

5. Think about the quotient of 0.056 ÷ 0.08. How many decimal places should there

   be in your answer? _____

   What is the quotient? _____

   How would you rewrite the problem and answer as fractions?

   _____

Show That You Know

Use the story and what you have learned about multiplying decimals and fractions to answer the following questions.

> In baseball, the "batting average" is one way to measure how good a player is at hitting the ball. To find a player's batting average, the number of successful hits a player has made is divided by the number of times the player has been at bat, and the result is written as a decimal. For example, if a player had 35 successful hits out of 100 times at bat, his or her batting average would be $\frac{35}{100}$ or 0.35.

1. Penny had 10 times at bat during her last three games. If she hit the ball successfully during five of those times at bat, what is her batting average for those games?

2. Eric had a batting average of 0.21 last season. What is his batting average this season if it is 1.4 times greater than last season?

3. What does a batting average of 1.0 mean? Write an example to demonstrate.

Show That You Know (continued)

4. How many times better is a 0.48 batting average than a 0.2 average?

5. You can multiply the batting average by the number of times at bat to find the number of successful hits. If a player had a batting average of 0.375 for 56 times at bat, how many successful hits did he or she have?

6. You can divide the number of successful hits by the batting average to find the number of times at bat. If a player had a batting average of 0.3 and 81 successful hits, how many times at bat did he or she have?

Review What You've Learned

7. What have you learned in this Connections lesson about the relationship between multiplying and dividing fractions and multiplying and dividing decimals?

8. What have you learned in this Connections lesson that you did not already know?

9. How will this lesson help you do math with fractions and decimals?

Review and Practice

Skills Review

Negative exponents:

If an exponent is negative, multiply the reciprocal of the base by itself the number of times shown by the exponent.

$$10^{-4} = \frac{1}{10} \times \frac{1}{10} \times \frac{1}{10} \times \frac{1}{10} = \frac{1}{10,000} = 0.0001$$

Rewriting scientific notation in decimal form:

If the exponent in the scientific notation is negative, move the decimal point to the left the number of places shown by the exponent.

$$6.1 \times 10^{-2} = 0.061$$

Rewriting a decimal in scientific notation:

Move the decimal point to the right and reverse the process for writing a number in scientific notation as a decimal.

$$0.061 = 6.1 \times 10^{-2}$$

Multiplying decimals:

Multiply the numbers as you would with whole numbers. Place a decimal point in the product so that the number of digits after the decimal point equals the total number of digits after the decimal points in the factors.

$$2.3 \times 0.35 = 0.805$$

Dividing a decimal by a whole number:

When dividing a decimal by a whole number using long division, place the decimal point in the quotient directly above the decimal point in the dividend.

Dividing a decimal by a whole number:

$$\begin{array}{r} 221.2 \\ 4\overline{)884.8} \end{array}$$

Dividing by a decimal:

If the divisor is a decimal, move the decimal point to the right until it is a whole number. Then move the decimal point in the dividend to the right the same number of places.

$$35 \div 0.5 = 350 \div 5 = 70$$

Strategy Review

- Finding patterns in numbers written in scientific notation and decimal form can help you rewrite numbers from one form into the other.

- Drawing a number line and making a list can help you use repeated addition to multiply a decimal by a whole number.

- The Guess, Check, and Revise Strategy can help you use multiplication to solve division problems involving decimals.

Skills and Strategies Practice

Write your answer to each exercise in the space provided.

1. Write the decimal for 3.6×10^{-3}.

_____

4. Write 0.00074 in scientific notation.

_____

2. Use a number line to find 0.2×5.

_____

5. Jo ran 4.41 miles over three days. If she ran the same amount each day, how many miles did she run in one day?

_____

3. Multiply 58.3×2.2.

_____

6. What is $398.44 \div 0.02$?

_____

TEST-TAKING tip

Remember to complete all of the steps for each calculation. For example, don't forget to place the decimal point in the product after multiplying decimals.

Unit Review

Circle the letter of the correct answer.

1. 3.2×10^{-3} is the same as _____.

    A. $32 \times 10,000$

    B. $32 \times 1,000$

    C. $32 \times (\frac{1}{10,000})$

    D. $\frac{1}{32} \times 10,000$

2. $0.33 \div 0.11 =$ _____

    A. 0.3   C. 3

    B. 0.0033   D. 0.03

3. 1.87×10^{-5} written as a decimal is _____.

    A. 0.0000187

    B. 0.00187

    C. 0.0187

    D. 18,700,000

4. $0.24 \times 0.024 =$ _____.

    A. 0.00576   C. 10

    B. 0.0576   D. 0.1

5. $179.358 \div 0.002$ is the same as _____.

    A. $17,935.8 \div 2$

    B. $179,358 \div 0.2$

    C. $179,358 \div 2$

    D. $17,935.8 \div 0.2$

6. 4.7×10^{-4} is equal to _____.

    A. $\frac{1}{47} \times 103$ C. 0.00047

    B. 0.047   D. 0.47

7. $0.048 \times 0.003 =$ _____

    A. 16

    B. 0.0144

    C. 0.00144

    D. 0.000144

8. $0.036 \div 0.12 =$ _____

    A. 0.0003   C. 3

    B. 0.003   D. 0.3

9. 0.03088 written in scientific notation is _____.

    A. $3,088 \times 10^{-2}$

    B. 308.8×10^{-2}

    C. 30.88×10^{-2}

    D. 3.088×10^{-2}

10. $10.75 \div 0.25 =$ _____

    A. 4.3   C. 2.6875

    B. 43   D. 26.875

11. $28 \div 0.093$ is the same as _____.

    A. $280 \div 9.3$

    B. $280 \div 93$

    C. $28,000 \div 93$

    D. $280,000 \div 9.3$

12. $0.9 \times 0.0018 =$ _____

    A. 50   C. 0.0162

    B. 500   D. 0.00162

13. 3.9×10^{-1} is equal to _____.

    A. 0.39   C. 3.9

    B. 0.039   D. $1 \div 3.9$

14. $12.24 \div 6 =$ _____

    A. 2.24   C. 2.04

    B. 0.204   D. 2.204

15. 0.00493 written in scientific notation is _____.

    A. 4.93×10^{-3}

    B. 4.93×10^{-1}

    C. 4.93×10^{-4}

    D. 49.3×10^{-1}

16. $600 \div 0.012 =$ _____

    A. 50,000   C. 50

    B. 5,000   D. 500

17. $0.135 \times 0.20 =$ _____

    A. 0.027   C. 0.0027

    B. 0.0207   D. 0.270

18. $308.9890 \div 1 =$ _____

    A. 308.8990

    B. 3.089890

    C. 30.89890

    D. 308.9890

19. 1.7×10^{-2} written as a decimal is _____.

    A. 0.17   C. 0.0017

    B. 0.017   D. 0.00017

20. $0.00015 \times 1.11 =$ _____

    A. 0.000165

    B. 0.0165

    C. 0.0001665

    D. 0.001650

21. 0.00000079 written in scientific notation is _____.

    A. 79×10^{-10}

    B. 79×10^{-9}

    C. 7.9×10^{-7}

    D. 7.9×10^{-6}

22. $51.34 \div 0.17 =$ _____

    A. 30.2   C. 302

    B. 3.02   D. 3.20

23. 10^{-2} is the same as _____.

    A. $\dfrac{1}{1000}$ C. 0.01

    B. 0.001   D. 1×10^{2}

24. $0.1 \times 0.20 =$ _____

    A. 0.002   C. 0.02

    B. 0.2   D. 0.21

Unit 4 Reflection

MATH SKILLS

The easiest part about multiplying and
dividing decimals is

The easiest part about dividing fractions is

Intense Sports

MATH STRATEGIES & CONNECTIONS

For me, the math strategies that work the best are

Decimals and fractions are related because

READING STRATEGIES & COMPREHENSION

The easiest part about previewing and predicting is

One way that previewing and predicting helps me with reading is

The vocabulary words I had trouble with are

INDEPENDENT READING

My favorite part of <u>Intense Sports</u> is

I read most fluently when

A

algorithm (AL-guh-rith-um): is a set of rules or a process for solving a problem (p. 31)

B

bar graph (bahr graf): a way of comparing information using rectangular bars (p. 18)

C

circle graph (SUR-kul graf): a graph shaped like a circle that shows a whole broken into parts (p. 18)

combination (kahm-buh-NAY-shun): a group of objects in which order does not matter (p. 8)

compatible numbers (kum-PAT-uh-bul NUM-burz): numbers that are easy to compute mentally (p. 61)

composite number (kum-PAHZ-it NUM-bur): a whole number that is greater than 1 with more than two factors (p. 104)

concept map (KAHN-sept map): a graphic organizer showing a main topic and related ideas (p. 10)

convert (kun-VURT): to change from one form to another (p. 202)

coordinate grid (koh-AWR-duh-nit grid): displays pairs of numbers (p. 18)

D

decimal (DES-uh-mul): a number that names part of a whole; has digits to the right of the decimal point (p. 68)

dividend (DIV-uh-dend): the number to be divided (p. 31)

divisible (duh-VIZ-uh-bul): a number that can be divided by a whole number evenly (no remainder) (p. 24)

divisor (duh-VY-zur): the number to be divided (p. 31)

E

equation (ee-KWAY-zhun): a mathematical sentence with an equal sign, =. An equation says that the side to the left of the equal sign has the same value as the side to the right (p. 79)

estimate (ES-tuh-mayt): to give an answer that is close to the correct answer (p. 61)

expression (ek-SPRESH-un): a mathematical statement including numbers and symbols (p. 4)

F

factor (FAK-tur): a whole number that divides another whole number with a remainder of 0 (p. 24, 104)

flowchart (FLOH-chahrt): a diagram that can be used to show the steps in a process (p. 10)

fraction (FRAK-shun): a form of a number that shows part of a whole (p. 68)

I

infect (in-FEKT): to introduce germs or viruses to someone or something (p. 116)

integer (IN-tuh-jur): a whole number (0, 1, 2, …) or a corresponding negative number (-1, -2, -3, …) (p. 221)

inverse operations (IN-vurs ahp-uh-RAY-shunz): operations that undo one another (p. 79)

invert (in-VURT): to reverse the positions of the numerator and the denominator of a fraction (p. 191)

L

long division (lawng duh-VIZH-un): the process used to break dividing multi-digit numbers into a series of easier steps (p. 239)

GLOSSARY continued

M

minuend (MIN-yoo-end): number or quantity from which another is subtracted (p. 148)

mobile (MOH-bul): able to move or be moved from one place to another (p. 116)

O

ordered pair (AWR-durd pehr): a pair of numbers that names one point on a coordinate grid (p. 18)

P

pattern (PAT-urn): objects, designs, or number that change in a specific way (p. 6)

perimeter (puh-RIM-uh-tur): the distance around the outside of a shape (p. 16)

physical model (FIZ-ih-kul MAHD-ul): a real-life representation of an object (p. 4)

place value (plays VAL-yoo): the value of the place where a digit appears in a number (p. 31)

plot (plaht): to find and mark the point named by an ordered pair (p. 18)

prime number (prym NUM-bur): a whole number with exactly two factors; one and the number itself (p. 104)

Q

quotient (KWOH-shunt): the answer to a division problem (p. 31)

R

reciprocal (rih-SIP-ruh-kul): the number that when multiplied by a given number, yields a product of one (p. 191)

remainder (rih-MAYN-dur): the number left over in a division problem (p. 68)

rounding (ROWND-ing): changing a number to the nearest ten, hundred, thousand, and so on (p. 61)

rule (rool): a description of the way a pattern works (p. 6)

S

scale (skayl): numbers that are the units used on a bar graph (p. 18)

scientific notation (sy-un-TIF-ik noh-TAY-shun): a way of writing very large and very small numbers as a number multiplied by 10 raised to an integer (p. 221)

simplify (SIM-pluh-fy): to re-write in an equivalent form that represents the simplest possible value (p. 111)

solution of an equation (suh-LOO-shun uv an ee-KWAY-zhun): any value or values that make an equation true (p. 79)

strategy (STRAT-uh-jee): a plan or way of doing something (p. 4)

subtrahend (SUB-truh-hend): the number that is subtracted from the minuend (p. 148)

T

three-column chart (three KAHL-um chahrt): a chart that can be used to take notes or organize ideas (p. 10)

tree diagram (tree DY-uh-gram): a diagram that shows possible combinations branching off each other (p. 8)

V

Venn diagram (ven DY-uh-gram): overlapping circles used to compare an contrast ideas (p. 10)